Lessons from the Bible

VOLUME 2: MATTHEW-REVELATION

THE REV. DEBRA MOODY BASS, PH.D

WESTBOW
PRESS®
A DIVISION OF THOMAS NELSON
& ZONDERVAN

WestBow Press books may be ordered through booksellers or by contacting:

WestBow Press
A Division of Thomas Nelson & Zondervan
1663 Liberty Drive
Bloomington, IN 47403
www.westbowpress.com
844-714-3454

ISBN: 978-1-6642-2102-4 (sc)
ISBN: 978-1-6642-2101-7 (e)

Print information available on the last page.

WestBow Press rev. date: 01/22/2021

This book is dedicated

To the loves of my life,

My son, Joshua D. Bass

And my Late Husband

Bishop Richard O. Bass, Sr.

CONTENTS

VI. APOCALYPTIC LITERATURE

INTRODUCTION

This is volume 2 *LESSONS FROM THE BIBLE: Matthew-Revelation.* Volume 1 focused on the books of the Old Testament: Genesis-Malachi. Volume 2 focuses on the books of the New Testament. *Lessons from the Bible – Volume 2* present each book of the New Testament and highlights three lessons from each book. The style is sermonic and can be read or preached to religious audiences across the globe. In addition, Sunday school lessons can be gleaned from the chapters and other avenues to teach and promote the word of God.

The New Testament was written over several centuries by many authors. It was influenced by various religious and philosophical teachings, encountered by the Christian community and oftentimes cultivated in order to make their message more relevant to its culturally different audiences.

Although the audiences changed over time, the gospel message remains the same throughout the New Testament – Jesus the Son of God was the Promised Messiah from the Old Testament, who came to save the world from its sins. This was accomplished through his virgin birth, his life of miracles and teaching, his crucifixion, and ultimately his resurrection. (*The Gospel of Matthew, RSV*) The story continues with the sending of the Holy Spirit on the day of Pentecost, *(Acts 2, RSV),* the following of new disciples: *Paul, Timothy and Titus to name a few (Acts 9, 16:1-3; Gal 2:1, RSV),* the conversion of thousands of Gentiles, the expansion of the ministry across the known world, and finally the birth of the Church.

However, the Church did not grow without controversy, division, and attacks on its founders. Eleven of the original disciples suffered violent deaths. Only John, the Beloved disciple, lived to a ripe old age. It was challenged from within by the community of believers and from without by rival religious, political, and philosophical groups. Yet through it all, the Church remained steadfast. In the words of Jesus, *"And the powers of death shall not prevail against it." (Mt 16:18, RSV)*

It is my prayer that as you read each lesson, you will be drawn closer to God and your heart and mind will be renewed in the words of truth that flow freely from each text. May God bless you and keep you is my prayer. AMEN!

THE FOUR GOSPELS

Matthew, Mark, Luke and John

Ain't No Mountain High Enough!

HOW DO YOU RESPOND TO A MIRACLE?

Matthew 17:1-5, *"And after six days Jesus took with him Peter and James and John his brother, and led them up to a high mountain apart. And he was transfigured before them, and his face shone like the sun, and his garments became as white as the light. And behold, there appeared to them Moses and Elijah, talking with him. And Peter said to Jesus, 'Lord, it is well that we are here; if you wish, I will make three booths here, one for you, and one for Moses and one for Elijah.' He was still speaking, when lo, a bright cloud overshadowed them, and a voice from the cloud said, 'This is my beloved Son, with whom I am well pleased; listen to him!'" (RSV)*

INTRODUCTION

The Gospel of Matthew is directed to a Jewish audience. He tries to prove to the Jewish people that Jesus was the Promised Messiah of the Old Testament. Matthew makes vv 1-13 (*Mt 17:1-13, RSV*) an instructional session for the disciples as well as his Jewish audience. For Matthew, Jesus stands in continuity with the revelation of the Old Testament to the Jews, symbolized in our text today by the presence of Moses and Elijah.

By portraying Moses, Elijah and Jesus talking together, Matthew confirms his view that Jesus is the fulfillment of the Old Testament promises made to Abraham, Isaac and Jacob. He has come now to fulfill God's will and work for all peoples and all eternity.

John the Baptist and Jesus the Messiah are the fulfillment of the Old Testament and now through their witness and leadership, future generations of believers will find and receive salvation. Salvation is now offered to all people, but a response is necessary. You must R.S.V.P.! This is the meaning of the story of the Transfiguration. Let us now examine the responses found in our text this morning.

1)

The first lesson teaches us that Peter, James and John had a ***SECULAR RESPONSE TO A DIVINE INTERVENTION.*** Read Mt 17:3-4, RSV *"And behold, there appeared to them Moses* *and Elijah, talking with him. And Peter said to Jesus, 'Lord, it is well that we are here; if you wish, I will put three booths here, one for you, and one for Moses and one for Elijah.'"*

According to tradition, the Transfiguration occurred on Mt. Tabor. Jesus takes his inner circle with him up to a mountaintop. In the Old Testament, retreating to mountains often triggered some type of spiritual experience or an encounter with God. After the vision was gone, they came down from the mountain. *(Mt 17:9, RSV)*

Just as soon as they arrived on the mountain, Jesus' physical nature is transformed and transfigured into a heavenly form glowing and shining brightly right before the disciples' eyes. They had never seen Jesus in this form before. It was obvious to them that something holy was going on, something terrifying, something powerful, and something mysterious.

One would think seeing Jesus transfigured into a ghost-like image would have been shocking enough! But suddenly, before they had time to adjust to Jesus' new form, here comes Moses and Elijah, joining him in the same transfigured ghost-like state of a heavenly being. All three were conversing on the mountaintop.

Now the three are in conversation with one another. The disciples are not privy to the conversation, but Peter decides that this reunion and gathering of the pillars of their faith need a secular response. It is interesting that they recognized Moses and Elijah, without Jesus having to introduce them to his inner circle. Perhaps when the transfiguration occurred, their spiritual awareness peeked, and their spiritual eyes were opened. The disciples were then allowed to enter a realm of the holy that is usually off limits to human, moral, and sinful beings.

Peter wants to give a response that he thinks is a good gesture to commemorate and celebrate the visitation of Moses and Elijah. His response is a secular, this worldly response. He wants to physically build 3 huts, or booths, or tabernacles – *shene* in the Greek – so the world would know what took place here.

But Peter's secular response was evidence that he misunderstood what had just occurred right before his very eyes! Perhaps he felt as the leader of the inner circle, he needed to do something, usually without much thought, just a knee-jerk reaction to commemorate this glorious encounter. It appears that the disciples never understood Jesus' actions and words until the resurrection. It was all about spiritual awareness, not secular tradition or wisdom.

Peter's response proved that he did not realize that Moses and Elijah were passing the baton of salvation over to Jesus. Jesus had fulfilled the Law that was given to Moses. Elijah appeared because Jesus had fulfilled the prophecies of the Old Testament prophets in relation to who he was and his role as the Lamb of God who takes away the sins of the world. We celebrate that in our Communion meal. Now it was all about Jesus and accepting his teachings as the final word and will of God.

When God sends a miracle in our lives, our response must be spiritual and not secular. When we respond spiritually, we send praises up to God and we acknowledge God as the source of our many blessings. We cannot give the devil or this world any credit. No matter how dark the night gets sometimes. Instead, let us respond to God's miracles by sharing the good news of God's love, grace, and mercy to the world – family, friends, co-workers, and church members - so the world will know that God, not man, is in charge. We do not need bigger or more Churches; we need a closer relationship with God and one another.

If you have received a healing from God respond to your healing miracle through witnessing and testimony. It was God who healed your disease. God may have used the doctors, nurses and hospital, but God supplied the healing. If you have received a financial blessing, respond to your financial miracle with your tithe and a testimony that God opened a window from heaven and poured out a blessing. If you found a new job, respond to your employment miracle by witnessing on the job that it was God who made a way out of no way.

So, every morning we should rise and shine and give God and God alone the glory. As children of the Most-High King, our response to God's miracles in our lives should always be a response of faith and not secular showboating.

----

2)

The second lesson we learn from the text is that the disciples should have chosen a ***DIVINE RESPONSE.*** Read v 5, *"He was still speaking, when lo, a bright cloud overshadowed them, and a voice from the cloud said, 'This is my beloved Son, with whom I am well pleased; listen to him!'"(Mt 17:5, RSV)*

Peter was so caught up in his secular response to the transfiguration that he almost did not notice the descending of a bright cloud that eventually overwhelmed the disciples. God interrupted Peter by appearing in a cloud. This was no ordinary rain cloud, but the heavenly cloud concealing the very presence of God.

From this cloud God spoke to the disciples. Jesus' identity was announced by the Shekinah glory as the unique Son of God. Jesus was not just one among three major figures of the faith. No, Jesus was and is the only voice and the only teacher that we are obligated to listen to. Moses is gone. Elijah is gone. Both were taken up to heaven by the hand of God. Only Jesus remained in the presence of the disciples.

God gave a direct command. There was no confusion over whom God was referencing. It was straightforward. God was authorizing his son is the only one who knows his will and does his will. This statement confirms that only Jesus has authority above and beyond Moses and Elijah.

You see, some of Matthew's audience believed Moses and Elijah were superior to Jesus. Matthew makes it very clear in this report that only Jesus has ultimate authority as the Son of God. God himself wanted them to know that the words of Jesus concerning the cross and resurrection were central to the good news of the gospel.

So now they needed to leave Moses and Elijah in the past and focus their attention on Jesus and Jesus alone. For Jesus fulfilled both the Law, which Moses represented, and the prophecies of the Old Testament, which Elijah represented.

As Christians, we know that our focus and attention is primarily on Jesus and his mission on earth to reconcile us to God. When we refer to the Old Testament it is not to give greater authority to the old dispensation or covenant, but rather to remind us of the efforts God went through to save us from eternal death!

Because we are Christians, we find our spiritual map and compass in the words of the New Testament. Here is where we learn about Jesus' birth, life, death, and resurrection. Here the New Testament informs us of the coming of the Holy Spirit that dwells with us now and will lead us to the Day of Judgment.

God spoke to the Jews in the Old Testament and now God speaks to all creation in the New Testament. In the New Testament we are given a divine response to the role Jesus played in God's plan for our salvation. We are told up front after his baptism, "This is my beloved Son, with whom I am well pleased." *(Mt 3:17, RSV)* And now we are told to listen to him.

Now in Matthew 17, we are commanded to listen to hear. *(Mt 17:5, RSV)* This command comes with an automatic response to "obey." For if you really listen, and hear Jesus' words found in the New Testament, it is obvious that obedience and hearing are two sides of the same coin. If you hear, you will obey.

Some people come to church every Sunday and never hear what God is saying to them. They brush off the sermon and say, "God's not talking to me. He is talking to somebody on another pew, in another church, but not me!"

No, God is talking to you! Listen! Open your heart and mind and really listen and feel his salvation. Listen and experience a transformation of your way of thinking and actions towards others. Jesus said on many occasions, *"He who has ears to hear, let him hear." (Mt 11:15, RSV)*

When we really listen to God's divine response a change will come over us. It takes a divine response to make our lives complete.

---

3)

Our next lesson teaches us that the only appropriate response to God's intervention in our lives is a **_WORSHIP RESPONSE._** Read vv 6-7, *"When the disciples heard this, they fell on their faces, and were filled with awe. But Jesus came and touched them, saying, 'Rise, and have no fear.' And when they lifted up their eyes, they saw no one but Jesus only." (Mt 17:6-7, RSV)*

The disciples were terrified. Fear after hearing the voice of God is a common experience in the Old Testament. When they heard the voice of God, they fell on their faces, in fear and worship. They recognized the nearness of God's presence and fell prostrate on the ground.

Fear is a common response to a manifestation or appearance of God in an unusual way. Yet, we must allow our fear of God to be channeled into our worship of God. When fear is channeled into worship, it becomes reverence and awe of the one who deserves our worship. Proverbs 1:7 states that *"The fear of the Lord is the beginning of knowledge." (RSV)* Peter may have responded incorrectly initially, but now he realized that it is about more than building booths and tabernacles, and new and bigger churches! It is about worshiping the Almighty God in whom we dwell and have our being.

At that moment, the disciples' fear was at its greatest, for they feared for their lives – man shall not see me (God) and live! *(Exo 33:20 RSV)* It was then that Jesus came to them when their fear overwhelmed them. The disciples are told to stop being afraid, and then Jesus touches them so they would know he was real, and not a ghost.

Once they felt his touch they looked up, and Moses and Elijah and God's Shekinah glory, were all gone! Only Jesus was left to bring comfort and encouragement to their fearful hearts. When life causes us to fear, let us remember the words of the Psalmist, *"I lift up my eyes to the hills. From whence does my help come? My help comes from the Lord, who made heaven and earth." (Psalm 121:1-2, RSV)*

At his touch all fear vanished. Jesus' touch signified a blessing – he was *"God with us."* That is what Emanuel means – *"God with us." (Mt 1:23, RSV)* It is Jesus alone who is God's tabernacle on earth – *shene*. Jesus is God's reality abiding with us now. Upon his physical departure, he sent the Comforter, the Paraclete, and the Holy Spirit, to dwell in our midst until his Second Coming – the *Parousia*.

Jesus is still reaching out to touch someone in need of a healing – both physically and spiritually. Only a touch from the Master can change us from the inside out. For when Jesus touches us, joy will flood our souls.

What is your response today to God's word and the miracles God has allowed to take place in your life? Is it a secular response like Peter's, ignoring the spiritual things that strengthen our relationship with the Father? Did you acknowledge that it was a divine response? If we do not respond correctly, when we experience the mountains in our life – trials and tribulations – they will overwhelm us and cause our faith to wither and fade.

Therefore, allow Jesus to respond to your needs by touching you where you need it the most? How will you respond? The correct response is a worship response. Let us then come and worship him, Jesus Christ our Lord!

THE GOSPEL OF MARK

The Cost of Discipleship

HOW MUCH DOES IT COST?

MARK 8:31-38, *"And he began to teach them that the Son of man must suffer many things, and be rejected by the elders, the chief priests, and the scribes, and be killed, and after three days, rise again." (RSV)*

INTRODUCTION

The Gospel according to St. Mark is the shortest of all the gospels. For this reason, it is believed to be the first Gospel written down. John Mark was a traveling companion of Paul, but later, after a disagreement, he joined Peter in Rome. It is believed by most scholars today, that the other gospels used Mark as a resource when they too decided to report on the life, death and resurrection of Jesus the Christ.

Mark's Gospel is obsessed with the *Messianic Secret*. This is the theory that the disciples never knew who Jesus really was, and that Jesus kept his real identity as the Son of God hidden, until after his death and resurrection. For almost in every instance where Jesus heals in Mark's Gospel, Mark has Jesus instruct them not to tell who had healed them. Even the demons were silenced.

Mark does not record the birth of Jesus. Instead, Mark records 13 occasions where Jesus healed the people. For Mark, this was proof enough that Jesus was the Son of God. Healings, not a virgin birth, were Mark's evidence of Jesus' true purpose as the Promised Messiah. The most important question for Mark is the identity question – Who is this man called Jesus and how much does it cost to follow him?

In chapters 8-10 Jesus prepares the disciples for the suffering they will undergo as his followers. The disciples' only understanding of the coming Messiah was that he would come as a great king and military powerhouse. This is what they had been taught from the Jewish prophecies about the Promised Messiah. When Jesus talked about suffering and dying, they were not able to accept the true cost of discipleship.

Our text today is the first prediction of the situation surrounding the cost of discipleship. Jesus teaches his disciples that there are three costs attached to true discipleship. Let us now examine these 3 lessons as we ask ourselves today, "How much does it cost?"

1)

The first lesson we learn about the cost of discipleship is ***SELF-DENIAL.*** Read v 34b, *"...If any man would come after me, let him deny himself and take up his cross and follow me." (Mk 8:34b, RSV)*

Self-denial was a major lesson that Jesus continually tried to teach his disciples. On one occasion he told them that *"Foxes have holes, and birds of the air have nests; but the Son of man has nowhere to lay his head." (Mt 8:20; Lk 9:58, RSV)* When Jesus sent his followers out in groups of two, they were instructed to take nothing with them except a staff, no bread, no bag, and no money in their belts. They were to depend upon the hospitality of strangers who heard and received their witness *(Mk 6:7-12, RSV)*. Jesus always traveled light. He understood the kind of problems that come from one having a need and love for an abundance of material things.

We see this in the eastern religions of Hinduism and Buddhism. These two religions teach that attachment to things bring suffering into one's life. Attachment to things can get in the way of you praising God. That is why Jesus said, *"It is easier for a camel to go through the eye of a needle, than for a rich man to enter into heaven." (Mt 19:24; Mk 10:25; Lk 18:25, RSV)*.

The disciples thought that following Jesus would eventually lead to positions of power and wealth. But had they understood what following Jesus really meant, that they would have to take up their crosses daily, whether they wanted to or not, and that they would have to suffer and die may have lessened the number of disciples that followed him.

Have you seriously asked yourself the question, *"How much does it cost to follow Jesus?"* If you think joining the Church will make you rich, think again! The true ministry of Jesus is about service and servanthood. That is why Jesus washed the disciples' feet in John's Gospel, to teach them humility and servanthood. *(Jn 13:5, RSV)* We should not ask to be served, but rather who can we serve?

The real question is what can I do for others? The late President John F. Kennedy said it best, *"Ask not what your country can do for you; ask first what you can do for your country."* So, if you start out with your hand out, looking to receive, the Holy Spirit will be absent from your life. For God gave his all to us when he sent his Son Jesus. We must now surrender our all to him.

God never promised us a rose garden, or a trouble-free life. If you choose to be called a Christian, you have a big target on your back for Satan's evil darts. Now you have chosen the way of the cross. This is how much it cost.

2)

The second lesson we learn about the cost of discipleship is that it costs you your ***SELF-WORTH.*** Read v 35, *"For whoever would save his life will lose it, and whoever loses his life for my sake, and for the sake of the gospel's will save it." (Mk 8:35, RSV)*

Jesus is foretelling his death and resurrection to his disciples. He is trying to explain the true cost of discipleship. The disciples were always concerned about those things that dealt with the physical life – food, drink, power, status, and money. Remember on one occasion Jesus said, *"And why are you anxious about clothing? Consider the lilies of the field, how they grow; they neither toil nor spin; yet I tell you, even Solomon in all his glory was not arrayed like one of these."* (Mt 6:28-29, RSV)

Jesus wants them to realize that if your life is primarily caught up with maintaining the physical being, and little attention is given to the spiritual dimension, you will soon lose focus, direction, and eventually your own soul. The logic behind this is that if you need a $50,000/ year job to maintain your current lifestyle, more than likely you will do whatever it takes to make sure you keep your job – whatever the cost or compromise!

The real question is really about allegiance. Where does your allegiance lie, and to whom? Can you be bought or sold, like Judas, for the right price? *(Mt 26:14-15, RSV)* You know they say we all have a price. What amount of persecution, torture, would make you curse God and die? Can I get a witness? Job lost everything: status, wealth, children, health, and friends. Yet he never gave up on God. *(Job 1:21)* Can you say this morning, "For God I live and for God I'll die?"

I did a study leave in Rome, Italy about 28 years ago. Part of our class requirement was to visit the catacombs, underground caves of the first Christians who were murdered for their faith in Jesus. Their persecution came under the Roman Emperors Nero and Julius Caesar. As I stood in this underground cemetery, I could feel the presence and testimonies of their lives. I was encouraged and moved to lift-up holy hands and my voice in praise of Almighty God.

My faith reached a greater depth on that day. I saw firsthand how much it cost to follow the Lord Jesus in a hostile world. The first Christians believed these words of Jesus, *"For whoever would save his life will lose it, and whoever loses his life for my sake will find it."* (Mt 16:25, RSV)

But how many of us would give our lives for Jesus and for the sake of the Gospel today? If the police came through the church doors one Sunday and arrested anyone who claimed to be a follower of the Way, for Jesus said, *"I am the Way, and the Truth and the Life; no one comes to the Father but by me."* (John 14:6, RSV) Who will stand up for Jesus? If you cannot stand up, no matter what the cost to you personally, then you are still struggling with the identity question: Who is Jesus and what does it cost to follow him?

Yet the Bible tells us clearly, *"For what does it profit a man, to gain the whole world, and forfeit his life?"* (Mk 8:36, RSV). That is how much it cost.

_____

3)

The third and final lesson we learn about what it cost to follow Jesus, is **_SHAME_**. Read v 38, *"For whoever is ashamed of me, and of my words in this adulterous and sinful generation, of him will the Son of man also be ashamed, when he comes in the glory of his Father with the holy angels."* (Mk 8:38, RSV)

Jesus was born into the 42nd generation counting from Adam. *(Lk 3, RSV)* This generation was a lost generation and had turned away from the true meaning of the Torah, the Laws of Moses. The temple was defiled because there were merchants who made an unfair profit, when people bought sacrifices in order to find forgiveness for their sins. *(Jn 2:14-16, RSV)* The true spiritual and redemptive understandings were lost, and the people were merely going through the motions. The Jews suffered much because of their disobedience to God's word. Even when they were under the punishment of God they still assimilated, compromised, and sold out to the religious and political cultures of their neighbors. *(Josh 24:14-15, RSV)* The consequence was a polluted and sinful generation, ashamed of the word of God.

They killed the prophets and they denied Jesus was the Messiah. They were ashamed of Jesus' lowly birth and existence. He was just a carpenter's son! Jesus hung out with dirty fishermen, prostitutes, adulterers, tax collectors, and Samaritans. *(Mt 9:10-13, RSV)* Jesus certainly did not act like a king!

So, who was this man? Can we trust him to do what he said he would do? If you are a Christian, that is a full-time position! You cannot resign when the going gets rough. You cannot retire when you feel you have had enough! No, no! Once you have put your hand to the gospel plough, there is no turning back. A plough can only go forward if it is going to be effective. It cannot go in reverse. If you turn back, you are not worthy of the Kingdom. *(Lk 9:62, RSV)*

So, I ask the question again. How much does it cost to serve the Lord? - all that you have, and then some. It requires your mind, body, and soul. Therefore, we must keep working and watching for the Kingdom. The cost by this world's standards may be too high, but the reward by God's standard is entrance into his Kingdom, to reign with him throughout all eternity. God bless you!

THE GOSPEL OF LUKE

A Mind Is a Terrible Thing to Waste

AN UNEXPECTED ENCOUNTER WITH JESUS

LUKE 8:26-39, *"Then they arrived at the country of the 'Gerasenes", which is opposite Galilee. And as he stepped out on land, there met him a man from the city who had demons; for a long time he had worn no clothes, and he lived not in a house but among the tombs. When he saw Jesus, he cried out and fell down before him, and said with a loud voice, 'What have you to do with me, Jesus, Son of the Most-High God? I beseech you, do not torment me.' For he had commanded the unclean spirit to come out of the man. (For many a time it had seized him; he was kept under guard and bound with chains and fetters, but he broke the bonds and be driven by the demon into the desert.) (RSV)*

INTRODUCTION

Luke draws this story from Mark's Gospel. He changed it somewhat to fit his own purpose and message about the power that Jesus possessed as the Son of the Most High God, and how this power was available to all who believed – both Jew and Gentile.

The theme of chapter 8 is two-fold: first to show the power of Jesus' words and second to reveal Jesus real identity, something the disciples still were confused about. *(Mk 4:41; 8:27-30, RSV)* The story is about a man, who was demon possessed, and his encounter with Jesus. This meeting eventually led to the return of the man's sanity. No longer could he be called disturbed. Now he was a disciple of Christ. Let us now listen to the lessons we learn from this text.

1)

The first lesson we learn from the text is that suggest you may be craze is **_WHEN YOU LEAVE YOUR COMFORT ZONE._** Read vv 26-28, *"Then they arrived at the country of the Gerasenes, which is opposite Galilee. And as he stepped out on land, there met him a man from the city who had demons; for a long time he had worn no clothes, and he lived not in a house but among the tombs."(Lk 8:26-28, RSV)*

This story takes place in Gerasa, the country of the Gerasenes, who were non-Jews or Gentiles. Gerasenes refer to persons living in an area on the east shore of the Sea of Galilee. The city was 6-7 miles inland and part of a league of 10 Gentile Greek-speaking cities known as the Decapolis (*meaning 10 cities*)

There were no crowds to meet Jesus and his disciples when they arrived on shore, as was usually the case. This is because they had left Jewish territory, their *comfort zone*. They were away from all the hassles and threats, attack and crying out for healing, that they encountered whenever they were on land back in Palestine.

Perhaps Jesus thought he was getting a break from all that attention, both negative and positive. He and his disciples got out of the boat and headed for shore not expecting what was about to happen next.

There is both the fear and the joy of leaving our *comfort zones*. We do not know what to expect. People usually want to stay close to home, to family, and to friends. Yet, never venturing out to see what the world has to offer us limits our progress and hampers our horizon. But if we decide to leave familiar grounds, people look at us with concern and think we have lost our minds!

Sometimes just choosing to go to college and not participate in the family business raises a red flag. Taking a job out of state or out of the country causes family and friends to wonder about your choices in life. Even changing denominations sometimes bring on the question, *"Where have we gone wrong?"* We have always been Baptist, or Methodist, Catholic, or Presbyterian.

Well the answer to this question is NO! You have chosen a different path for your life and are marching to the beat of a different voice inside of you. God has planted a seed in your life, and you must follow wherever that spark leads you, even if it means leaving your *comfort zone*. Jesus moved around, as he felt led by the Spirit. *(Lk 4:16-19, RSV)* Sometimes we are in places of comfort; sometimes we are in places of conflict. Jesus met the demon-possessed man when he went out of his *comfort zone* and into Gentile territory.

What does God have in store for you when he calls you to leave your *comfort zone*? A new job? A new partner? A new degree? A new home? Is there a board or organization you could be on serving God, but instead you choose to lose out because you are not comfortable working with people who do not look or act like you? Has God put a ministry or message on your heart, but you do not feel comfortable taking the lead? My advice to you then is take courage! Let go of your *comfort zone* and let God. Say in the words of the prophet Isaiah, *"Here am I, send me." (Isa 6:8, RSV)*

----

2)

Secondly, people will challenge you **_WHEN YOU BELIEVE IN THE POWER OF GOD._** Read vv 28-31, *"When he saw Jesus, he cried out and fell down before him, and said with a loud voice, 'What have you to do with me, Jesus, Son of the Most High God?' I beseech you, do not torment me.' For he had commanded the unclean spirit to come out of the man. (For many a time it had* *seized him; he was kept under guard, and bound with chains and fetters, but he broke the bonds was driven by the demon into the desert.)(Lk 8:28-31, RSV)*

Luke does not tell us how the man ended up in this situation. But it was believed that demons could enter your body at any time. *(Lk 11:24-26, RSV)* He fell before Jesus when the demons recognized Jesus as the Son of the Most-High God. Luke reports that they begged Jesus not to torment them. *(Lk 8:3, RSV)* The man probably was tormented over the years by the townspeople who would capture him and bind him with chains and shackles. When the demons saw Jesus, they assumed Jesus was going to do the same thing – torment him. But he was so wrong. You see the demons believed in the power of God. The demons that were making this man act violently and exhibit destructive behavior were afraid of the power that the Son of God had over them. *Lk 8:6-7, RSV)*

Perhaps somewhere inside this man was his true self and when he saw Jesus, he believed in him, based on the witness of the demons living inside of him. As he began to believe, his faith was causing the power of Jesus' spoken word to heal him and perform an automatic exorcism.

Maybe if the demons had been quiet, the man would not have known who Jesus was. After all, he was not a Jew! But because of their witness to his identity, the man now believed in the power of God! Probably for the first time in a long time, he saw hope for his miserable condition.

Jesus was able to look inside this man's soul through his eyes. For "the eye is the lamp of the body." *(Mt 6:22, RSV)* Then Jesus asked him, "What is your name?" *(Lk 8:30, RSV)* It was believed that one had dominion over that which you name. *(Gen 1:26-28; 2:19-20, RSV)*

Do you remember when you were a child and your mother caught you doing something you should not have done? If you were not close enough for her to grab you, you heard your whole name loudly voiced across the room or throughout the neighborhood. She would call your first, middle and last name in one breath. You knew then you were really in trouble. Just hearing your name made you straighten up and do the right thing.

The demon-possessed man told Jesus that his name was Legion. Now a legion was a Roman army consisting of 6000 men. That is a whole lot of demons in one body. No wonder the man possessed such strength.

The text tells us that Jesus spoke and commanded the unclean spirits to come out of him. When the demons begged Jesus not to send them to the abyss – a place where disobedient spirits were imprisoned - but instead, allow them to go into the herd of pigs on the hill beyond, their request was granted. Asking to be sent into a herd of pigs reminds us of the Jewish culture of holiness surrounding this story: pigs are unclean; they could not have contact with the dead or they were unclean. All were to be avoided at all cost, less you to became labeled "unclean" by the priests and removed from borders of society. *(Lev 11; 13, RSV)*

So, for Jesus to even talk to this man meant he was risking (yet again) being labeled as "unclean". Yet Jesus' main concern was for the man, not the pigs! Believing in the power of God is crucial to making things happen in your life.

Do you believe in a God that today many people question even exists? Perhaps. Do you believe in the power of God when God has brought you from a mighty long way? Maybe. Is it problematic to believe in the power of God if everything else you have tried has failed? Well it depends on whom you ask. But if you ask *Abraham*, a friend of God, he will say, "Trust in God!" *(Gen 12, RSV)* If you ask *Jacob* who ran from his brother for 20 years, then forgiven for the theft of his brother's birthright and blessing, he will say, "Trust in God!" *(Gen 33:1-4, RSV)*

If you ask *Joseph*, whose brothers sold him into Egyptian slavery because they were jealous of him, if you are making a mistake believing in an all-powerful God, he will say, 'NO!" *(Gen 37:25-28, RSV)* If you ask *Moses* who met God on a mountain and was handed the 10 Commandments, he will say, "Try God!" *(Exo 20, RSV)* If you ask King *David*, who faced Goliath when no other soldier would, he will say, "Believe in God's protection!" *(1Sam 17:48-51, RSV)* And the roll call goes on and on.

What about you today? Do you mind being called zealous for the Lord?

_____

3)

Our final lesson from this text that proves putting your trust in God is a sound and wise decision is **_WHEN YOUR TEST BECOMES YOUR TESTIMONY._** Read vv 37-39, *"Then all the people of the surrounding country of the Gerasenes asked him to depart from them; for they were seized with great fear; so he got into the boat and returned. The man from whom the demons had gone begged that he might be with him; but he sent him away saying, 'Return to your home, and declare how much God has done for you.' And he went away, proclaiming throughout the whole city how much Jesus had done for him." (Lk 8:37-39, RSV)*

After the demons entered the pigs, they went wild, and the demons in them became self-destructive as they had been when they were inside the man. So, the pigs got to running and ran right off the cliff into the water, and since pigs cannot swim, they all drowned, causing a great financial lost to the owners of the herd.

A whole herd of pigs that were being raised for profit, to be sold in the local marketplace for food, was destroyed. The men that were caring for the swine were amazed, confused, and scared out of their minds. They ran into town to tell the people about how a Jew came and destroyed their pigs! Now you know that did not go over too well in Gentile territory, where eating pork was a daily occurrence. Just think if you could not eat any ribs or pork chops or neck bones, or bacon, honey baked ham, chitterlings, you get the point.

The townspeople probably were in a mob mode and came out to see this troublemaker and how they could get rid of him. When they got there, what they witnessed was astonishing! The demon-possessed man was sitting clothed and quiet at the feet of Jesus. No chains, or shackles.

Who was this powerful man? What else will he do to us? He has to leave our area immediately and leave us alone! Be gone with him. Jesus did as they requested. Jesus never wants to be where people will not receive him. So, he and his disciples got back in their boat and ready to return to their *comfort zone.*

Afraid of what might happen to him once Jesus was gone, the now healed man asked Jesus if he could come with him. Jesus said no! You see Jesus does say no sometimes. Why did he say no to this man's request to follow him back to Palestine? Because he had a testimony that needed to be heard by all those who wanted Jesus gone. This man's test was enduring 6000 demons within his body. His testimony was that he was free of demons and he was now a disciple, appointed by Jesus to go home and be a witness for him.

He was to tell everybody what God had done for him. Confused? Yes, he was for a little while. But now he can tell the world and show the world how the Lord made a difference in his life.

Do you trust God enough to be a witness for Jesus? Are you committed enough to remain steadfast through life's trials and tribulations, through sickness, through foreclosure, through unemployment, through bankruptcy, through the death of a loved one, through the abandonment of family and friends, and even through covid-19? Then stand up and be a witness! The world is longing for evidence of God's love, God's mercy, God's forgiveness, and God's healing touch.

God is offering you a new life, eternal life, a life in service to him. This seems scary to the world and unbelievers when you step out of your *comfort zone*. However, the blessings that come as a result of your stepping out on faith will be amazing.

As believers we go where we are sent depending on the power of God to go with us. Does that make people question our decisions? I do not mind at all. How about you?

THE GOSPEL OF JOHN

A Party With a Purpose

LET THE PARTY BEGIN!

JOHN 2:1-4, *"On the third day there was a marriage at Cana in Galilee, and the mother of Jesus was there. Jesus also was invited to the marriage with his disciples. When the wine gave out, the mother of Jesus said to him, 'They have no wine.' And Jesus said to her, 'O woman, what have you do with me? My hour has not yet come'"* *(RSV)*

INTRODUCTION

When folk hear the word "party", they immediately attach a worldly connotation to it. Webster's College Dictionary defines a party as, *"a group gathered for some special purpose or task."* (Random House Webster's College Dictionary, N.Y., 1997, p 951) Now that sounds to me like another definition for the Church! Are we not a group of people gathered for some special purpose – to worship God, and to have a task - to establish God's kingdom on earth and proclaim salvation to all who dare believe? Well then, **LET THE PARTY BEGIN!**

In our text we read that Mary was already at the wedding reception by the time Jesus and his disciples arrived. They showed up on the third day of the wedding. Jewish weddings usually lasted 7-10 days. Jesus was delayed because he was in the city of Bethsaida, busy making fishers of men, calling disciples to take part in bringing the kingdom of God here on earth.

Now the party was in full swing. Everybody seemed to be having a great time when suddenly Mary, the mother of Jesus, notices the wine was almost gone. The story does not tell us why the wine supply ran low. Perhaps some guests who neglected to RSVP decided to show up and their presence created a shortage.

Or maybe it was one of those real hot days in Israel when the shade was over 100 degrees, and everybody was extremely thirsty. But whatever the reason, John tells us that it was Mary who took it upon herself to solve the shortage problem. Is it not just like a woman!

But why was this the case? Why did Mary make this problem her problem or more specifically, why did she make it Jesus' responsibility to correct it? Well, the jury is out on why according to many scholars. Some say it was the wedding of a close relative of Mary, maybe even one of her stepchildren she inherited when she married Joseph. Others say that she was the host or wedding coordinator. Still others speculate that Mary was trying to force the hand of Jesus by making Jesus reveal his special powers before it was his time to shine. There was a commercial slogan that said, *"We'll serve no wine before its time."* Perhaps this was Jesus' spiritual position.

Then there is the notion that this is really a metaphor explaining the relationship of Christ to the Church, and how Christ provides the cleansing agent for sinners, which is the wine we share in communion.

I believe this story has 3 vital lessons for today's Church. So, **LET THE PARTY BEGIN!**

_____

1)

The first lesson we learn is that ***JESUS IS THE ONLY OPTION TO SALVATION.*** Read v 6, *"Now six stone jars were standing there, for the Jewish rites of purification, each holding twenty or thirty gallons." (Jn 2:6, RSV)*

The Jews were caught up in rituals involving washing in water that was marked holy or blessed. But in God's eyes, water alone was no longer good enough to wash away their sins, their unrighteousness. Jesus' entrance on the scene now provides a new cleansing agent that washes away all sin – past, present, and future.

Jesus is the new way to salvation. John the Baptist bore witness to it in the first chapter of John *(1:33)*, and Nicodemus is given a crash course in it in the third chapter *(3:2-5)*. The wedding at Cana is placed in between these two chapters to provide evidence of the power and connection between Christ's coming, and the salvation his ministry, death and resurrection has given to all of us. Jewish purification rites were just empty practices and had no power to forgive sin.

You see water leaves the stain of sin in our hearts. But Jesus' blood bleaches the stain clean through forgiveness and redemption. Tide cannot get it out. Gain cannot get it out. Oxyclean cannot get it out. Clorox cannot bleach it out. Nothing but the blood of Jesus can turn us into righteous vessels to be used by God for his service. So, **LET THE PARTY BEGIN!**

_____

2)

The second lesson we learn in our text is that ***WE MUST SHARE OUR NEW FOUND SALVATION WITH OTHERS.*** Read vv 7-8, *"Jesus said to them, 'Fill the jars with water.' And they filled them up to the brim. He said to them, 'Now draw some out, and take it to the steward of the feast.' So, they took it." (Jn 2:7-8, RSV)*

Jesus gives the stewards orders to fill these water jars with water, which were used for the Jewish purification rites. They obeyed Jesus since Mary had given them strict orders to do whatever he told them to do. It would be nice if we were that obedient.

Then Jesus said to them, *"Now draw some out, and take it to the steward of the feast."* So, *they took it. (Jn 2:8, RSV)* These stewards did not understand what was going on. They thought they were taking water to the chief steward to drink. They were only following orders. What happened along the way was not of their doing. The water miraculously was transformed into wine via the power of the Holy Spirit, and thanks be to God the Holy Spirit still today is transforming our communion meal of bread and wine into the powerful saving blood of Jesus!

The stewards took the water to the chief stewards according to Jesus' instructions. We too are instructed to share our cup of salvation and the good news about what the blood of Jesus can do for you to everybody we know. Our testimonies should be fresh and current, not 40 years old! For Jesus blesses us every day. It is not about the big things God has done for you, but the everyday, little blessings that we take for granted.

God did not have to wake us up this morning. God did not have to give you the use of your 5 senses, your limbs, and your bodily functions. God is good all the time and all the time God is good! Even when we are struggling, and in despair, we know we can turn to God in prayer. We know that we have salvation because God loved us so much that he sent his only Son. *(Jn 3:16, RSV)* There are no prerequisites required. Only faith in a risen Savior! You do not have to have a college degree, a million dollars in the bank, your skin can be whatever color God made you, and still you are blessed and highly favored. All you need to know is that salvation is in the cup!

All you do is to come to the party and receive joy, unspeakable joy. Jesus' death eliminated the religious rituals that would block our path to God. The stewards did not know what would be in that cup. The wedding needed more wine so that is what was in the cup 2000 years ago. What do you need more of today? Do you need more love in your life? It is in the cup! Do you need more power? It is in the cup! Do you need healing? It is in the cup! Do you need a financial blessing? It is in the cup! Do you need more peace? It is in the cup! Just drink today and *let the party* begin in your life.

_____

3)

Our final lesson from this text is that ***JESUS HAS THE BEST WINE IN TOWN!*** Read vv 9-10, *"When the steward of the feast tasted the water now become wine, and did not know where it came from ….the steward of the feast called the bridegroom and said to him, 'Every man serves the good wine first; and when men have drunk freely, then the poor wine; but you have kept the good wine until now.'" (Jn 2:9-10, RSV)*

After the stewards presented to the chief steward what they assumed was water, they were surprised to hear him exclaim that what they had brought to him was the best wine of the day! The chief steward congratulated the bridegroom on his strategy, for everyone was well aware that the host of any party presented the best wine first while the guests were sober, and their tongue pallets could detect the good quality of the wine. They would tell everyone after the party was over, how great or how bad the wine was at the event.

Then after the guests were intoxicated, and their tongues were numb, the host would pass out the cheap stuff without anybody noticing the difference in the quality of the wine. The

Laws of Moses were the first batch of wine that got the Jews intoxicated over their special status as God's chosen people. But due to their disobedience and idolatry, it was no longer enough to save them, and it was rendered null and void. The people could not keep the law and threw all righteousness to the wind. *(Micah 6:6-8, RSV)*

What does this say to us today? God sent Jesus to us while we were still able to say, "yes" to salvation. Jesus has come as our Savior today. Later Jesus will come as our judge. Jesus knows that we are intoxicated by the sins of the world and that the only way we can be delivered is to receive the best wine in town – which is salvation through his shed blood.

Jesus came all the way down through 42 generations to make us spiritually sober. *(Lk 3:23-38, RSV)* Spiritually sober means to obey God's word, to walk in God's ways, to love one another as God has loved us. Do not get drunk off this world's temptations and desires. The devil will offer you all this world has to offer in exchange for your soul. *(Mk 8:36, RSV)*

You can get sober. The world's place to get sober is AA. But I am offering you J.C. – Jesus Christ. You can change your brand of wine. Just take a drink of Jesus. He is the best wine in town. *"O taste and see that the Lord is good! Happy is the man who takes refuge in him!"* (Ps 34:8, RSV)

Are you ready for the party to begin? Then take a drink today and be made whole again. God bless you!

THE ACTS OF THE APOSTLES

THE BOOK OF ACTS

The Church is Born!

GOD'S TKO!

ACTS: 9:1-9, *"But Saul still breathing threats and murder against the disciples of the Lord, went to the High Priest and asked him for letters to the synagogues at Damascus, so that if he found any belonging to the Way, men or women, he might bring them bound to Jerusalem. Now as he journeyed, he approached Damascus, and suddenly a light from heaven flashed about him. And he fell to the ground and heard a voice saying to him 'Saul, Saul, why do you persecute me?'..." (RSV)*

INTRODUCTION

I was a big boxing fan back in the days of Muhammad Ali, Sugar Ray Leonard, Leon Spinks and Mike Tyson. Boxing is a sport where you must anticipate your opponent's every move. You must stay fit, move quickly, and throw a powerful punch in the early rounds if you want to score points and win the fight. However, sometimes both opponents fight well, and nobody gets knocked out. Then the judges tally their scores, who won how many rounds, and the fighter with the most points is declared the winner by a technical knockout (TKO).

The game of life is sometimes like a boxing ring. Every round brings new challenges, some expected, some unexpected. The very time you think you are winning – Pow! - You get knocked down or you are up against the ropes, trying to stay in the game. Sometimes your physical injuries are unbearable.

But you keep hanging in there swinging with everything you have, hoping to land a powerful enough punch to knock out your opponent. Our opponent is Satan, the devil, who is trying to take us out in the early rounds of life but because of the blood of Jesus, he goes the whole 15 rounds! Then at the end, God will determine the winner.

In our text Paul is the evil power that seeks to destroy the followers of the WAY, the initial title for followers of Jesus. They were called followers of the WAY because Jesus proclaimed in John 14:6, *"I am the way, the truth and the life..." (RSV)*

Luke now begins a new section of his account of the Acts of the Apostles. From here on in, Luke focuses on the man Saul, a Pharisee and persecutor of the WAY, who was converted and given a new name, Paul. His new job was Apostle to the Gentiles and defender of the faith. *(Acts 22:21, RSV)* This conversion and change of heart happened because of God's TKO. Let us learn from the word of God.

———————————

1)

As we read our text, the lesson that immediately stands out is that in order to experience God's TKO, ***WE MUST FIRST KNOW THAT THE ENEMY IS CONSPIRING AGAINST US!*** Read vv 1-2, *"But Saul still breathing threats and murder against the disciples of the Lord, went to the High Priest and asked him for letters to the synagogues at Damascus, so that if he found any belonging to the WAY, men or women, he might bring them bound to Jerusalem."* *(Acts 9:1-2, RSV)*

After Jesus' resurrection and ascension, the Pharisees and Sadducees thought that all the hoopla and noise surrounding the man Jesus would die down. However, that was not the case with everybody. Saul, a devout Pharisee, would not rest until every person – man, woman, boy, or girl, were brought to justice for having believed in the man Jesus.

Saul's anger had not subsided. Rather his anger grew daily. So much so that the scriptures say he was *"breathing threats and murder against the disciples of the Lord."* *(Acts 9:1, RSV)*

Have you ever let something, or someone get you so angry that smoke was coming out of your ears, so to speak? You were so mad you could not see straight! This is how Saul felt about Jesus and his disciples.

Saul was so angry that he went seeking permission to go hunt down some followers of the WAY who had escaped to Damascus. They were called followers of the WAY before they were called Christians at Antioch. But it was Saul's intention to get in their way!

You see Saul had either captured, killed, or run out of town most of the believers. Yet the thought that some of them got away just burned in his heart and mind. Paul wanted to extend his authority across the border to Damascus to pursue his hatred for these disciples and possible fugitives from Jerusalem.

Now Damascus was the oldest city in Syria about 140 miles from Jerusalem. It was not under the Roman rule, so Saul needed to use religious authority to go to Damascus. The Sanhedrin Court had jurisdiction over all synagogues, no matter where they were located. Therefore, Saul received religious papers to go to the Jewish synagogues to arrest any followers of Jesus and bring them back to Jerusalem to stand trial.

As believers we must remember that the enemy is always conspiring against us, trying to break our spirit, set us up in a lie, destroy our integrity, embarrass us in the presence of others by questioning our words and actions. Jesus reminds us, *"If the world hates you, know that it hated me before it hated you."* *(John 15:18, RSV)* But he also said, *"In the world you have tribulation; but be of good cheer, I have overcome the world."* *(John 16:33, RSV)* In other words, our enemies cannot do any more to us than God allows. And when your test is over, God will shut down the enemy and restore what you lost.

God does not want us to be naïve, thinking everybody will love us and support us. Instead, God wants us to do the right thing no matter what the consequences or what the enemy throws at us. Daniel and the three Hebrew boys are witnesses to how our enemies set traps to destroy us, but they are defeated because God covers us with his protection. *(Dan 3:19-23; 6:10, RSV)* David said it so well: *"Even though I walk through the valley of the shadow of death, I fear no evil; for thou art with me; thy rod and they staff, they comfort me."(Ps 23:4, RSV)*

No, you are not paranoid if you think people are out to get you because the devil is on his job 24/7. Just know God's got you and he will TKO your enemies.

_____

2)

The second lesson we learn as we continue to examine the text is that **_GOD WILL RESPOND TO THE ENEMY'S PLAN OF ATTACK._** Read vv 3-5, *"Now as he journeyed, he approached Damascus, suddenly a light from heaven flashed about him. And he fell to the ground and heard a voice saying to him, 'Saul, Saul, why do you persecute me?' And he said, 'Who are you Lord?' And he said, 'I am Jesus whom you are persecuting.'" (Acts 9:3-5, RSV)*

What was about to happen to Saul was his worst nightmare. He was arrogant and proud because he had received letters from the high court to arrest those in Damascus. Then suddenly he is knocked to the ground, by God's TKO, in the form of a flash of bright light and a voice from heaven. Now the descent from Mt. Hermon, where Paul was, to Damascus, goes through a region well known for violent electrical storms. But this was no ordinary lightening; it was a supernatural noonday experience.

Here he was, strong and powerful, well trained in the Old Testament scriptures, yet he had no clue as to who the Messiah really was. Jesus had to first get his attention. Saul was familiar with how divine beings appeared on earth with a bright light that shown all around them for the light was necessary to veil the face of God, for no one can see God's face and live.

The bright light was designed to startle Saul, get his attention, and show him who Jesus really is. This bright light flashed like a lightning bolt during a major thunderstorm. The light shone all around him, not just in front of him. On every side he turned, the light of Jesus was there. There was no escaping his power.

Out of respect and awe, he fell to the ground, as did all those with him. Then Jesus' voice spoke calling him by name, *"Saul, Saul, why are you persecuting me?" (Acts 9:4, RSV)* You see wherever the glory of God is shown, a word from God is heard. Well Saul had no clue what the voice was talking about. He had always defended the law against all false attacks. That is why he was on his way to Damascus in the first place!

Then Saul asked the voice to identify itself. *"Who are you Lord?" (Acts 9:5, RSV)* Again, Saul is oblivious to the voice of God; he has no clue what is going on. The prophet Isaiah's experience is similar in his vision of God. Most of his life, Isaiah was a court prophet, working for King Uzziah. He did not really know the Lord. *(Isa 6:6, RSV)* Like Judas' betrayal of Jesus, after working and living with him for 3 years, he did not know Jesus' real identity, or mission.

(Mt 10:4, RSV) So, it is with the Church, you can come Sunday after Sunday and not know the Lord on a personal level.

Paul retells the event with additional words from Jesus in Acts 26:14: *"Saul, Saul, why do you persecute?" It hurts you to kick against the goads"* *(RSV)* When Jesus uses the word persecute here, he means pursuing or driving away his believers. For when you attack them, you attack Jesus. The Bible says, *"Touch not my anointed ones; do my prophets no harm!" (Psalm 105:15, RSV)*

Jesus could not tolerate Saul's actions against his followers any longer. Saul had to be stopped. His misguided mission needed to be shut down. Yet Jesus decides not to kill him – that is showing mercy – but to change his heart and make a believer out of him with God's TKO. Now that is grace!

Here we have Saul, a Jew, converted in Gentile country, to be an Apostle to the Gentiles, the people he despised the most. That is God's TKO. His whole spiritual world was turned upside down. What was gain will become loss; what was honor will now be lifelong shame and a permanent blot on his character. He will be viewed as a traitor to the Jews, not fit to be called a Pharisee.

God reacts the same way in our lives. God knows what you are going through, and because God loves you, God will respond to the enemy's plan of attack on your life. Then God will make your enemy a footstool. *(Acts 2:35, RSV)*

When the *Sauls* in our lives come after us, God already has a plan in place and in gear that will give us the victory. Either God will change the heart of the enemy, or God will subdue them with a TKO. Either way, we will be blessed in the end. We will be able to proclaim God's deliverance from our foes. God's faithfulness will see us through our every danger, toil and snare, because his grace is sufficient, and it is amazing.

God is awesome and Saul, who after this conversion experience, used the name Paul, learned his lesson the hard way, that God's TKO will make a difference in your life if you go against his will. Paul was moved from self-centered independence to total dependence on the Lord and his fellow disciples.

Therefore, as believers, let us not think too highly of ourselves. *(Rom 12:3, RSV)* You do not want to be a candidate, like Paul, for one of God's TKOs.

----

3)

Our final lesson learned from this text is that ***YOU MUST FOLLOW DIRECTIONS AND STAY IN HIS WILL.*** Read vv 6-9, *"But rise up and enter the city, and you will be told what you are to do. The men who were traveling with him stood speechless, hearing the voice, but seeing no one. Saul arose from the ground; and when his eyes were opened, he could see nothing; so they led him by the hand and brought him to Damascus. And for three days he was without sight, and neither ate nor drank." (Acts 9:6-9, RSV)*

Paul was humbled and his whole demeanor changed. The big and bad persecutor, standing less than 5 feet tall according to some accounts was now submissive to the authority of the resurrected Savior. In his current blind condition, he had enough sense to follow the Lord's directions, *(Acts 9:6 RSV)"* Jesus had to bring Paul to his knees so he could teach him and then restore his sight. The famous slave trader of the 1800s, John Newton, wrote after his conversion to Christianity, *"I once was lost but now am found, was blind but now I see. (AMAZING GRACE HYMN, 1725-1807)*

Those with Paul heard his voice but they were not privy to the resurrection vision of Christ. You see the light without the vision, the Spirit and the grace, is not enough to convert you. Many Christians are drawn to the light, but they have not surrendered their lives and hearts totally to Christ. For the Bible tells us, *"For many are called, but few are chosen."* (Mt 22:14, RSV)

Afraid and confused, they got up and rode into Damascus according to the instructions Jesus gave to Paul. Paul was probably weak and had to be helped up. Through this vision God performed a TKO. Paul realized he had just experienced a divine revelation and felt the need to respond through prayer, meditation and fasting. He was no longer his own, now he belonged to God.

In other words, he wanted to be completely in tune and ready for whatever Jesus was going to show him in Damascus. Paul let go of any preconceived notions that he was in charge. Now he humbly submitted his will and his life over to Jesus. Jesus accepted Paul's repentance, and cleaned up Paul's heart for the new role he was to play in God's plan of salvation as an Apostle to the Gentiles. The Bible says, *"So faith comes from what is heard"* and Paul heard and obeyed the voice of Jesus. *(Rom 10:17, RSV)*

Paul's new message to the world is that we are saved by faith and faith alone! *(Gal 2:15, RSV)* It is not about the law! It is not about where you come from or who your ancestors are. It is not about your gender. It is not about your social position. It is about believing that Jesus is the Promised Messiah, rose from the dead and is the Son of the Most-High God.

This faith breaks down all barriers that humanity has put in place. Jesus' death on the cross put an end to all of that. On the cross, God performed his greatest TKO against sin and eternal death. Jesus conquered the law as our judge. He revoked and cancelled the original sin that we inherited from Adam and Eve. He brought down divisions of all kinds and levels. Then finally Jesus paid the cost for eternal death, *"for the wages of sin is death, but the free gift of God is eternal life."* (Rom 6:23, RSV)

Back in the 70s, there was a Broadway musical entitled, *"YOUR ARMS ARE TOO SHORT TO BOX WITH GOD."* Well, nothing has changed! Our enemy's arms are still too short to box with God and win. For the Bible teaches us, *"No weapon that is fashioned against you shall prosper."* (Isa 54:17, RSV)

Remember when we are under attack by opposing forces of every kind, these 3 steps will lead us to the victory: stay focused by pressing forward; follow the directions and commandments of God; and love and forgive one another as God has loved and forgiven us. Never try to defeat your enemy using human tactics of vengeance, gossip, and violence. Jesus says, *"But I say to you, 'Love your enemies and pray for those who persecute you.'"* (Matt 5:44, RSV). Then let us move on and worship God in both spirit and truth. *(Jn 4:23, RSV)* God bless you!

THE LETTERS OF PAUL

The Disputed and the Undisputed

THE LETTER TO THE ROMANS

(Undisputed!)

I Am My Neighbor's Keeper!

ALL FOR ONE, AND ONE FOR ALL!

ROMANS 15:1-6, *"We who are strong ought to bear the failings of the weak, and not to please ourselves; let each of us please his neighbor for his good, to edify him. For Christ did not please himself; but as it is written, 'The reproaches of those who reproached thee fell on me.' For whatever was written in former days was written for our instruction, that we by steadfastness and by encouragement of the scriptures, might have hope. May the God of steadfastness and encouragement grant you to live in such harmony with one another in accord with Christ Jesus, that together you may with one voice glorify the God and Father of our Lord Jesus Christ." (RSV)*

INTRODUCTION

When I read this scripture – Romans 15:1-6 – the first thing that came to my mind was the famous cry of the Three Musketeers, *"All for One and One for All!"* These three sword-fighting men of war did not allow the bond they had with one another to be broken by any means – internal or external. They faced death together on numerous occasions defending country and the right. This was a book published in 1844 by Alexander Dumas.

The phrase, *All for One and One for All,* implies that all members of a group support each of the individual members and the individual members pledge to support the decisions of the group. This is the sentiment of our text for today.

The Epistle or Letter to the Roman Church is the most commanding exposition of the gospel of salvation by grace through faith. It is Paul's longest letter and outlines his theology and understanding of God and his Son, Jesus the Christ. Paul writes the letter near the end of his third and final missionary journey. It is believed that he dictated the letter to his disciple, Tertius, while in the Greek city of Corinth.

The letter is written to a Church that Paul neither founded nor visited prior to sending this letter. Some believe Roman Jews, who were present at the Pentecost explosion in Acts 2, started the Church. Now they were filled with the Holy Spirit and returned to Rome and shared the good news they heard from Peter's sermon at Pentecost. From their testimony alone, the Church in Rome was born.

Paul writes this letter because some tension was brewing in the Church there. The original Jewish founders were run out of town by the Roman Emperor Claudius, which left the Gentiles in power and control of the Roman Church. *(Acts 18:1-2, RSV)* After Claudius' death, the Jews returned home to find their old positions now filled by Gentiles. This caused tension between the Jews and the Gentiles, thereby motivating Paul to write this letter for two reasons: first, to introduce his perspective on the gospel; secondly, to promote harmony in Christ, welcoming all believers into the fold.

Harmony among all believers is still a battle being fought in Christendom today. Yet, Paul gives us a prescription that will help us avoid the trap of division – ***ALL FOR ONE, AND ONE FOR ALL!***

Now let us hear the lessons from our text.

_____

1)

The first lesson we learn is found in the first part of our title, **_ALL FOR ONE!_** Read v 1, *"We who are strong ought to bear with the failings of the weak, and not to please ourselves." (Rom 15:1, RSV)*

The Church in Rome existed maybe 10 years before Paul sends this letter. Some of the members were still *"infants in Christ,"* a phrase Paul used in I Corinthians 3:1. *(RSV)* The original Jewish founders were steeped in the Old Testament traditions and rituals and were accustomed to the ceremonies of baptism and the Lord's Supper performed a certain way. They were probably supporters of the phrase, *"We've always done it this way!"*

They had organized the Church the way they saw fit and had a low tolerance for any Gentile influence on the rituals. But because Jews had been expelled from Rome earlier, the new Gentile converts ran the Church the best way they knew how in their absence. Perhaps even incorporating some of their old ways of idol worship.

Perhaps some rituals were added or deleted from the traditional rituals and practice. Or maybe a new flair to the Old Testament ritual allowed Gentile believers to embrace the service on their terms, not having the advantage of proper instruction from the Torah or Law of Moses. All they wanted to do was to praise the Lord! To lift the name of Jesus! To testify what a change faith in Jesus had made in their lives!

Maybe they did not administer the Lord's Supper the same way as was previously done by the Jewish leaders. Maybe they quoted a scripture wrong. Maybe the order of worship was modified. Maybe the Apostle's Creed was left out of the service. Whatever failings the strong witnessed in the weak, Paul says put up with it! *(Rom 15:1, RSV)*

Correct do not criticize. Teach, do not bully or judge. *(Rom 2:1, RSV)* God shows no partiality! *(Rom 2:11, RSV)* Be an example through love, which encourages, supports, teaches, and gently corrects. *All for One and One for All!* We are all servants of Christ! Just as Jesus bore our weaknesses and took them to the cross, we are commissioned through Jesus to do the same for one another.

The Bible says love covers a multitude of sins. *(I Peter 4:8, RSV)* So as Christians, as followers of the Christ, let us embrace one another in love. For it is only in love that we find strength to bear one another's burdens. *All for One and One for All!*

2)

The second lesson we learn is the later part of the phrase: **_ONE FOR ALL!_** Read vv 2-3, *"let each of us please his neighbor for his good, to edify him. For Christ did not please himself; but it is written, 'The reproaches of those who reproached thee fell on me.'"* (Rom 15:2-3, RSV)

Paul went on three missionary journeys, sharing, teaching, and preaching the Gospel message as he received it on that memorable day on the road to Damascus. After being knocked to the ground and blinded, he continued to Damascus to meet with Ananias, who restored Paul's sight. Ananias, the leader of the WAY in Damascus, taught Paul the Gospel message. *(Acts 9:17-19, RSV)*

But it was as if Paul received a new vision, had new eyes. Not the old eyes of a pharisaic persecutor of the Church. New eyes that had seen the resurrected Lord! This was a one on one personal opportunity to be forgiven.

Paul immediately began to preach Jesus in the synagogues. Yet he knew he was still an Apostle in training and still had much to learn. So, he spent in the time Arabia – his seminary training - before he felt strong enough to take on the world. *(Gal 1:17, RSV)*

You see before you can help somebody you have to first be sure you are right with God. You must fasten the *belt* of truth around your waist. You must put on the *breastplate* of righteousness. You must wear the *shoes* of the gospel of peace, not Luis Vuitton or Jimmy Choo, or red bottoms. Then take your *shield* of faith, which will help quench the evil darts of the evil one. You must place the *helmet* of salvation upon your head. Then you must carry the *sword of the Spirit*, which is the Word of God. *(Eph 6:14-15, RSV)*

It is not until we are fully dressed in the whole armor of God, that we are equipped to enlighten and encourage those who are weaker in the faith. Otherwise, it will be the blind leading the blind.

It is never about you and me. It is always about others and how we can bring them to God. We must not edify ourselves but edify the community of believers. For Christ is our example. You are one person, but you must decide if you are part of the problem or part of the solution.

Jesus said *"for I was hungry and you gave me food, I was thirsty and you gave me drink, I was a stranger and you welcomed me, I was naked and you clothed me, I was sick and you visited me, I was in prison and you came to me…And the King will answer them, 'Truly, I say to you, as you did it to one of the least of these my brethren, you did it to me.'"* (Mt 25:35, RSV) *ALL FOR ONE AND ONE FOR ALL!*

3)

The final lesson Paul teaches is that **_HARMONY IS SUSTAINED THROUGH CHRIST._** Read vv 5-6, RSV, *"May the God of steadfastness and encouragement grant you to live in harmony* *with one another, in accordance with Christ Jesus, so that together you may with one voice, glorify the God and Father of our Lord Jesus Christ." (Rom 15:5-6, RSV)*

Paul was asking a strange thing. He was suggesting that the strong and the weak (who have disagreed on some things) now speak with one voice and with one mind in order to glorify God. Paul knew that Christian harmony is a gift of God's steadfastness and encouragement. This allows believers to share a united outlook, and together glorify God. *(Eph 4:5, RSV)*

Verse 5 is a prayer for the people to live in harmony. Unity between the weak and the strong can be achieved according to the principle of Christ, by welcoming one another, just as Christ has welcomed each of us.

Harmony comes when men and women, boys and girls, the educated and uneducated, young and old, black and white and yellow and red, stand in one accord for Jesus. One accord for Christ means in agreement with God's will for our lives, and for the life of the Church.

Harmony balances out the sounds of discord and selfishness. Harmony puts back in tune those voices that are out of tune, always wanting their own way and not God's way or what is best for all the people. Harmony makes sure every beat is brought in line and only the harmonious rhythm of God's people can be heard.

For example, when the black keys on the piano are played, the white keys wait for their turn to chime in and create the harmony that makes music pleasing to our ears. The black keys know they need the white keys. The flat notes know they need the sharp notes, so the sound is united. If you try to play only the flat notes or only the white keys, the sound is disturbing and unpleasing to the ear. The flat notes are sometimes viewed as weak in sound. The white keys, however, always support the black keys because without them, their sound would be off key, and the piano would not ring true to its existence.

So too is it with the Church. Some members are stronger than others, but that does not make them better! It just makes them more responsible for the weaker members. You are only as strong as your weakest link (member?). That is why we need each other because we are all a part of God's family.

Putting Christ first, allows us to agree to disagree without hatred, and vengeance in our hearts. In Phil 2:5, Paul says, *"Have this mind among yourselves which is yours in Christ Jesus."(RSV)* Christ's mind was always focused on others – healing others, saving others, feeding others, teaching others, and finally dying for others and rising from the dead for others, you and me, so we would have a chance at eternal life.

When the world sees we cannot get along with each other, how is God glorified? A divided house cannot stand! United we stand, divided we fall. Therefore, the strong must relinquish certain things they are free to do, for the sake of the weaker member. We are our neighbor's keeper!

If like Paul you are the stronger one, then reach out to the weaker one and pull them up, encourage them, support them, teach them, pray with them until they too can be called strong in the faith and love of our Lord and Savior, Jesus the Christ. For in Christ there is not big "I" or little "You".

So let us come together as one and glorify God so that souls may be saved. Jesus said, *"And I, when I am lifted up from the earth, will draw all men to myself."(John 12:32, RSV)* Yet, we can only lift up Jesus when we come together as one. ***ALL FOR ONE AND ONE FOR ALL!*** Amen!

I CORINTHIANS

(Undisputed!)

Witnessing Through the Broken Body and Shed Blood

LIVING WITNESSES

I CORINTHIANS 11:23-26, *"For as often as you eat this bread and drink the cup, you proclaim the Lord's death until he comes." (v 26, RSV)*

INTRODUCTION

In the 11ᵗʰ chapter of Paul's first letter to the Corinthians, Paul encounters many problems relating to the communion services held in the Church in the city of Corinth. As usual, Paul tries to address the issues according to their particular time frame, the church's situation, and the cultures directly involved. It was not easy. Yet even though Paul tried to be all things to all people his good intentions sometimes backfired.

In a town like Corinth, almost identical to the seashore town of Atlantic City, New Jersey, or Mobile, Alabama, there were many differences among the peoples of all nationalities and religious backgrounds. Paul's method would undoubtedly step on somebody's toes, eventually. He then appealed to their newly found Christian belief and uses that as a common denominator.

Paul tries to set up a standard by which Christians could live, a religious guideline for the partaking of the Holy Communion. Paul thought this was imperative because Christian unity was essential if one is to be a witness for Christ, living witnesses to the event of his death and resurrection.

This for Paul was the major function of the early Church. Witnesses going forth into all the world, never counting the cost nor looking for gain, but witnesses whose very essence of being is to proclaim the good news, to tell others about this miraculous event. *"For as often as you eat this bread and drink the cup, you show the Lord's death until he comes." (I Cor 11:26, RSV)*

In other words, every time you partake in this communion service, you are witnessing to the fact that the Messiah has already come. We are not waiting like the Jews. Here is a declaration, which has no rival. *"You proclaim the Lord's death as often as you drink and eat this." (I Cor 11:26, RSV)* And in showing his death, which is a gift of life to sinners, we witness in threefold the gospel message.

But how do we give witness to Jesus' death and resurrection by partaking of the communion meal? Well, let us listen and hear a word from the Lord for our own lives.

1)

The first lesson we give witness to **_SHOWS OUR OBEDIENCE TO CHRIST._** Read v 24, *"And when he had given thanks, he broke it, and said, 'This is my body which is for you. Do this in remembrance of me.'" (I Cor 11:24, RSV)*

Paul writes to the Christians at Corinth because of their disobedience to the memory and mandate of Jesus himself. They have come to the communion celebration with divisions in their hearts – some had food, some did not. Some had drink and some did not. They did not share. Those who had, ate and drank, and left nothing for the poor who had to work late. *(I Cor 11:20, RSV)* Certainly, this could never happen in the Church today!

The result was animosity, suffering, hunger, jealousy, anger, doubt and fear – all these emotions were being brought to the communion table because Jesus told the disciples, *"Do this in remembrance of me." (I Cor 11:24, RSV)*

The emotional and spiritual conditions that existed in Corinth were very similar to those experienced around the table of the Last Supper. Those 12 disciples were full of fear, jealousy, doubt and anger. But even knowing this about these 12 men, whom Jesus loved for 3 years, he still commanded them to do this in remembrance of me. *"For as often as you drink this cup, you proclaim the Lord's death until he comes." (I Cor 11:26, RSV)*

Paul reminds the Corinthians of this, and he reminds us today. God knows what is in your heart and your mind when you come to the table. You can fool the pastor, and members, but you cannot fool God! Yet the Church must be responsible and obedient to Jesus' command – *"Do this in remembrance of me."(I Cor 11:25, RSV)* So in response to this command and out of gratitude and obedience, we come to the table.

Yes, we come! With all our problems, aches and pains, with all our histories and past sins. But whatever our condition, still we come. Why? Because Jesus calls us to the table and out of obedience we come. For Jesus knew that what this table has to offer can cure whatever problem you bring to the table.

If it is a financial problem – come! If it is difficult relationships – come! If you have lost your job – come! If you suffer with health problems or all the above, come! The blood of Jesus can wash it all away. The blood that gives us strength every day, and new mercies every morning, shall never lose its power over sin.

Communion is for the living! When we experience the power of the shed blood and the broken body, we then become living witnesses for him.

2)

The second lesson we learn as living witnesses is that **_WE ACKNOWLEDGE THE DEATH AND SACRIFICE OF JESUS._** Read the second part of v 26, *"You proclaim the Lord's death…" (I Cor 11:26, RSV)*

The Corinthian Church was caught up in doing its own thing. Paul says to them in v 20, *"When you meet together, it is not the Lord's Supper that you eat." (I Cor 11:20, RSV)* Paul was focusing on the Corinthians real reasons for coming together. It was not to celebrate and remember that Jesus died for their sins. They were celebrating for other reasons, for selfish reasons, for social reasons, distinguishing between the rich and the poor. It was an occasion to flaunt their wealth and status in the community. It had nothing to do with Jesus' sacrificial death.

So why do you come to the table? Do you come because it is expected of us? Do you come because you are afraid somebody might talk about you if you do not come to the table? Communion Sunday is usually the Sunday when everybody comes to Church. It is the Sunday when we gather at the altar, eat the bread, drink the wine and have the slate wiped clean for the next 31 days.

We get to start all over again every Communion Sunday! It is like the year of Jubilee. We are declared without sin by the blood of Jesus. Last month's mistakes are gone, forgotten, and cast into the sea of forgetfulness. Not by any magic wand or hocus pocus, but by the shedding of the blood of the Lamb.

Communion reminds us that Jesus died for our sins and that his blood is our cover, our refuge, and our defense. When we pick up that wafer, which represents his broken body on Calvary, we should not be thinking, "O how much longer is service going to be?" We should not be thinking "O boy, tomorrow is a workday, what am I going to wear?" We should not be thinking, "I sure hope I do not have to kneel next to her?"

Instead, what we should be thinking is how mighty is our God! What we should be saying is our salvation is connected to the blood of Jesus. For you see the mind cannot get right until the heart gets right. If we feel gratitude and love and thanksgiving and redemption in our hearts, then our minds will join in the praise and celebration. Then we can come happy to the communion table because we will know the truth and the truth will make us free. *(Jn 8:32, RSV)* Living witnesses – what are you a witness to today?

_____

3)

Our third and final lesson from this text teaches us that when we witness through communion, **_WE BELIEVE JESUS IS COMING BACK._** Read the last part of v 26, *"…until he comes"* (I COR 11:26, RSV)

The Corinthian Church was so concerned about this world, the here and the now, getting their bellies full of wine, that they tainted the communion service. They thought it was only about them disagreeing, only about them getting along. But Paul reminds them of the bigger picture: that this ritual is only temporary until the Lord returns. *(I Cor 11:26, RSV)*

Therefore, they must agree and be on one accord now. They must forgive one another and put away all their differences when they come to the communion table now. If they fail to do this now, they will bring eternal destruction upon their own souls.

Have we forgotten that we are only doing this until the Lord returns? Are we so comfortable in the ritual that we are just going through the motions? Do you envision the broken and beaten body when you take the bread? Do you see the shed blood running down his pierced side, and his thorn pressed forehead when you take the cup?

This is all temporary! It is just for a season! It is only a practice to keep our hearts in tune until our Savior comes back looking for a Church without a spot or blemish. When Jesus comes back, we will not need communion to remember his sacrifice. He will be here in person in all his glory. Then the altar we will gather around will be the one in heaven as they begin to crown him King of Kings and Lord of Lords. *(Rev 17:14, RSV)*

Do you want to be a witness now so you can be counted as a member of his family later? Do you want to be a witness now, so you can hear him say, *"Well done, good and faithful servant; you have been faithful over a little, I will set you over much; enter into the joy of your Master."* *(Mt 25:21, RSV)* Then you must be a living witness today, right now, and not wait until tomorrow. Once Jesus is back, it will be too late.

If you have not been obedient, start now. Start now proclaiming the death of Jesus as the salvation for the whole world. Do not be ashamed of him and what he has done for you. If you are ashamed of him down here, Jesus will be ashamed of you before his Father. *(Lk 9:26, RSV)*

Why then is it important to be a living witness until Christ's return? - Because somebody does not believe. Somebody thinks this world is all there is and nothing else exists. But communion denounces that position. Communion shouts to the world with the loudest cry, "For I know my redeemer lives!" *(Job 19:25, RSV)*

Communion gives hope to a dying and sin sick world. It provides security from an eternal hell. It obtains freedom for the captive. Oh yes, as oft as we do this, we show the Lord's death; we remind others of God's love for them and to them. But most of all we proclaim that he is coming back! Jesus' death proved how much God loves us. Has God's love lifted you today? Then be a witness for him! God bless you!

II CORINTHIANS

(Undisputed)

Having The Right Attitude

AN ATTITUDE OF GRATITUDE

II CORINTHIANS 9:6-15, *"The point is this: he who sows sparingly will also reap sparingly, and he who sows bountifully will also reap bountifully. Each one must do as he has made up his mind, not reluctantly or under compulsion, for God loves a cheerful giver. And God is able, to provide you with every blessing in abundance, so that you may always have enough of everything, and you may provide in abundance for every good work." (RSV)*

INTRODUCTION

Paul established the Church in the city of Corinth on his first missionary journey. There were many problems within the Church, but the main problem was division among the members. The rich members thought they were superior to the poor and working-class members. They tried to bring the world's social and economic divisions into God's house. Paul let them know without a doubt that in Christ we are all equal – no male or female, no rich or poor, no young or old.

During Paul's early years as a traveling missionary, a famine due to drought, severely affected the lives of the Jewish Christians who lived in Jerusalem. Paul thought it God's will for him to contact all the Gentile Churches he had founded, requesting their immediate financial assistance to help alleviate the suffering of the poor. *(I Cor 16:1-3, RSV)*

Many of Paul's Churches were amenable to the idea and quickly responded to the call for help. Not so much with the Church in Corinth. The Corinthians had initially agreed to give assistance, but when they fell out with Paul, decided to hold back on their financial gift. Our text is Paul's response to their lack of support of those less fortunate and in need.

Let us now listen as Paul attempts to persuade the Corinthians that blessings come, when you learn what we need in order to have an attitude of gratitude and be blessed.

1)

Paul's first lesson reveals to us that there is **_A LAW OF GIVING._** Read v 6, *"The point of this: he who sows sparingly will also reap sparingly, and he who sows bountifully will also reap bountifully."(II Cor 9:6, RSV)*

The Corinthians had not learned how to give and help others. They seem to have feared that such giving might lead them to suffer want later. Paul's first lesson to them and others who thought that way, is the *law of giving.* What is the *law of giving*? The law of giving states that God will prosper those who are generous and give them the financial means to continue to help others.

Paul asked that monies be given systematically, on a regular basis, so there would be no pressure to collect an offering when he arrived. You see the rewards of giving are in proportion to the degree of your generosity. Limited giving equals limited blessings. God is able to reward his people and will reward generous giving with abundant spiritual and material prosperity, so that the giver can give even more!

It is like the story of Elijah and the widow who gave her last measure of meal and oil to feed the prophet of God during a drought. Because of her faith and obedience to the prophet, her food and oil supply never ran dry. *(I Kings 17:8-16, RSV)* The reward of generosity is a generous heart, which rejoices in giving and seeks nothing in return.

God blesses us not to be selfish, like the man who had full barns and instead of sharing what he had, tore down the old barns to build bigger barns. Little did he know that on that same night his soul would be required of him and his riches would be given to others. *(Lk 12:16-20, RSV)* Instead, God gives to us so we may do good works and be a blessing to others. This is the *law of giving* that only works if you have an attitude of gratitude.

2)

Paul's second lesson to the Corinthians in support of generous giving places focus on how we feel when we give – that is called the **_ATTITUDE OF GIVING._** Read v 7, *"Each one must do as he has made up in his mind, not reluctantly or under compulsion, for God loves a cheerful giver." (II Cor 9:7, RSV)*

Paul was aware of the source of the Corinthians' stinginess. They had fallen out with him because of the lies his enemies were spreading about him and his message, misrepresenting the good news of the gospel in Jesus Christ. When Paul was in their midst for 18 months, they worked with him, they accepted his teaching about justification through faith and faith alone, that salvation is free.

He taught that they did not have to become Jews first, before they converted to Christianity. But now Paul had moved on to Ephesus to work with the Church there. He believed they were sound and that his teaching had penetrated their hearts and taken root. So, he felt comfortable to leave the Church in the hands of those who he appointed leaders in his stead.

Yet, just as soon as Paul left town, his enemies, the Judiazers, who taught salvation must come through the Torah *(the first 5 books of Moses – Genesis-Deuteronomy)*, followed Paul to Corinth to confuse the new converts and make Paul out to be a liar and a fraud.

In the middle of all this Church mess, a decision was made not to send the money. Some who still supported Paul wanted to give if only to keep their word, not so much to help the poor in Jerusalem. Since all the other Churches were contributing to the collection, they did not want to look bad, even if they were not giving it from the heart. But for Paul, giving must be wholehearted. Giving should be done with a cheerful spirit. Giving is the fruit of wholehearted service and generosity. It is the companion of unselfish love.

When it comes time to give, our own needs may appear more pressing but that is a mirage of Satan. For Satan knows if he can keep you from giving your tithes and offerings, he can block your blessings. When the blessings are blocked, life becomes a struggle. Peace leaves the mind. Doubt and fear take over and thanksgiving is replaced with mumbling and stinginess. A loving and generous spirit will reap a harvest of love and kindness. David said in Ps 37:25, *"I have been young, and now am old; yet I have not seen the righteous forsaken or his children begging bread." (RSV)*

Giving is an act of faith to which God responds. Think about the farmer. He plants his seeds in the ground believing that the ground, with help from the rain and fertilizer, will produce a harvest at harvest time. The farmer trusts God to do what God does – cause his investment to grow. The same law of increasing returns operates in the law of giving.

Instead of being afraid that tithing will somehow decrease our bank accounts, we should rely on God to supply our needs. Our blessings do not come from a job, but from our heavenly Father. Jobs come and go. Only God is a sure thing. This is an attitude of giving.

---

3)

Paul's final lesson on giving in the Church leads us to how we respond to all that God has given to us – this is the ***GRATITUDE OF GIVING.*** Read vv11-12, *"You will be enriched in every way for great generosity which through us will produce thanksgiving to God for the rendering of this ministry not only supplies the wants of the saints, but also overflows with many thanksgivings to God."(II Cor 9:11-12, RSV)*

Paul argued that the collection was not for their glory, but so that the glory of God might be revealed to those in need who in return would be thankful. It is Paul's hope that their generosity may serve to overcome the prejudices between Jews and Gentiles and build instead a bridge of fellowship between them, even though Jerusalem was so far away. Paul believed the collection is the Corinthians opportunity to show how the gospel has won their hearts. It is a test of their spirit.

As Christians, tithing is the test to show how deep and developed our love and faith is towards God and one another. When we tithe it is a victory of love over selfishness. When we tithe the storehouse of God is full. When the storehouse is full, ministries that can reach out to the community can be financed. Then, our outreach will show God's love to others through us.

Sure, the government has programs, the state has programs, and the city has programs. But their messages are secular, not glorifying God. What is God's Church doing to help alleviate some of the ills within the community where we live? Are we helping children learn to read and write? Are we helping adults develop social and economic skills to live within their budgets and means? Are we teaching parenting skills to teenage mothers? No. Why? - Because there is no money available to do ministry that will bring others to Christ. Why? - Because God's people have not responded generously to the Psalmist's question *"What shall I return unto God for all his bounty to me?" (Ps 116:12, RSV)*

The answer is an *attitude of gratitude*. When we stop and think about the goodness of the Lord how can we not give the tithe? The tithe is not about the pastor, what denomination you belong to, or who you are mad with this week. The tithe is about thanksgiving to God for gifting us his Son Jesus the Christ. It is about God allowing the sun to shine on the good as well as the wicked. It is about God allowing you to live another day. Tithing is about your relationship with God. No more, no less. If we love God, then we tithe, not grudgingly, nor of necessity, but out of love for him.

When grace is received, it demands a response. The grace that comes from God to us finds its completeness as it flows through us towards others. But material blessings are not all that God gives to us. We ought to also be grateful for our spiritual blessings. Jesus said in the famous Sermon on the Mount, *"Do not lay up for yourselves treasures on earth where moth and rust consume, and where thieves break in and steal; but lay up for yourselves treasures in heaven where neither moth nor rust consumes…" (Mt 6:19-21, RSV)*

These are spiritual blessings. Good things follow us spiritually when we relate to God financially. Giving in worship is not a temporal matter only – this worldly – but it is an eternal act that registers in heaven.

Giving in church does much more than just pay the bills. Giving gives us credit in our spiritual account. It would be a shame to save all our money here in an earthly bank, die and leave it to somebody else to spend. Then you get to heaven and find out your spiritual account has been closed and stamped non-sufficient funds!

Having an attitude of gratitude fills up our spiritual bank accounts and preserves our place in glory. We give because we are thankful, grateful, appreciative, responsible as well as accountable. Yes, we love God. Yes, we love Jesus. Then let us put our money where our mouths are by possessing an attitude of gratitude. God bless you.

THE LETTER TO THE GALATIANS

(Undisputed)

Fruits Of The Spirit

GOD'S FRUIT MARKET

GALATIANS 5:22-23, *"But the fruit of the Spirit is love, joy, peace, patience, kindness, goodness, faithfulness, gentleness, self-control: against such there is no law." (RSV)*

INTRODUCTION

The theme for the 1993 Week of Prayer for Christian Unity was ***Bearing the Fruit of the Spirit.*** It was based initially on some texts prepared by the Kinshasa ecumenical group of Zaire, Africa. The illustration for the Week of Prayer for Christian Unity was an icon painted by a Russian in the 15th century. The icon is an interpretation of Abraham's hospitality in Gen 18, when the Lord appeared to him as 3 persons representative of the divine community, which serves as a model for human community. This theme was pregnant with imagery and creative possibilities for interpreting the work of Christ that has begun within those of us who give witness to the salvation that we experience because we have accepted Jesus Christ as Lord and Savior over our lives.

The verb "to bear" is used in the present tense in order to present a continuous action form – ***bearing*** – implying that the fruit of God's Spirit requires some response on our part. It denotes productivity, not passivity. The Spirit within us does not lie dormant until we are called home to glory, but it calls us to action. Bearing fruit is visible evidence of our connection to Christ's death and resurrection. For Jesus said, *"…for the tree is known by its fruit." (Mt 12:33, RSV)* Therefore, when we bear the fruit of the Spirit, whose we are becomes obvious to all.

Today's message is titled, ***GOD'S FRUIT MARKET.*** When I read the theme, I immediately began to envision the produce section of a grocery store. I am a lover of fresh fruits and vegetables and nutritionists have determined that at least 5 fruits and vegetables a day helps prevent all forms of cancer from developing in your body. I was a vegetarian for 10 years and never felt better in my life. Fruit not only tastes good, but it carries nutritional value essential for human beings to maintain healthy bodies and thus, healthy lives.

Just as earthly tangible, eatable fruit is good for the body, God's fruit market is good for our souls. Paul lists 9 things that give witness to the power of the Holy Spirit working in our lives: love, joy, peace, longsuffering, gentleness, goodness, faith, meekness, and self-control.

(Gal 5:22-23, RSV) As I read this long list, I can see immediately what areas I still need to work on in my own life in order that my witness might be complete.

When we visit God's fruit market, we discover 3 categories of fruit that play an essential role in maintaining healthy spiritual lives, that enhance our relationship with God and our neighbor, and that contribute to the goal of realizing Christian unity in our lifetime. These 3 categories of fruit must be incorporated in the institutional Church if we are ever going to achieve Christian Unity. This is the message Paul tries to relay to the Galatians who are divided on grounds of both race and religion.

_____

1)

The first category of fruit that we learn a lesson from in God's Fruit Market is called ***PASSION FRUIT.*** Read v22 a, *"But the fruit of the Spirit is love, joy, peace..." (Gal 5:22, RSV)*

Paul and I have a lot in common. Wherever we are, controversy of some sort seems to follow us because we are so passionate about God's plan of salvation for a dying world. The Gentile Christians living in Galatia were new converts and inexperience in the types of rituals and sacraments that were second nature to the Jewish Christians.

Paul tried to teach them that faith in Jesus Christ was the only initiation they needed to receive salvation. But his opponents, and even the other disciples, saw the Gentiles differently from themselves. After all, they were considered heathens, savages, uncultured. They chose racism, classism, and other dividing categories, instead of passion, to label those who were different, but also a part of the body of Christ.

So, conflict and confrontation erupted, and they began fighting and devouring one another. There was a breakdown of love and unity among those who were in power and those who were without power. For those who were in power wanted the new converts to act just like them! The kinds of demands the Jewish and cultic religious leaders were making on the new Gentile converts, was evidence that there was no *passion fruit* within and between the religious communities.

This category of the Spirit includes ***love, joy and peace.*** *(Gal 5:22a, RSV)* Having possession of these 3 fruits in our lives reflect what Christian Unity is all about. For you see God's love has been passed down to the Church from the cross. The Church then is responsible for passing on this same love and passion to every neighbor, to every stranger that we encounter all in the name of Jesus.

This agape love of God is not an erotic love *(eros)* but an unconditional love that says it does not matter who I am, what color my skin is, what gender I am, what size I wear, God still loves me passionately, and we as God's Church must transmit that same unconditional love to those in our communities – without exception! Until the Church learns to love unconditionally, there can be no Christian Unity. *(I Cor 13, RSV)*

Yet, when we do love unconditionally, oh what joy bubbles over in our souls. Joy is included in the ***passion fruit*** section because when we learn to love all peoples, then the joy of the Lord oozes out of every part of our existence. People will then want to come back to the Church or join for the first time because they will not be judged or violated or humiliated – they will feel the love that radiates from the Church whose ministry is filled with joy.

The Christian Church should be about joy, unspeakable joy. It should be heard from the rafters on Sunday morning, it should be rung from the bell towers and steeples, it should be preached from the pulpits, it should be prayed in the prayers, sung by the choir. If the Church reclaims the joy of the Lord, which is our strength, Christian Unity will soon become a reality. *(Neh 8:10, RSV)* Once we accept and give love, the joy of knowing nothing can separate us from the love of God dictates **peace** of mind. *(Rom 8:35, RSV)* This is the last of the **passion fruits.**

Life is so full of uncertainties and if it were not for the Lord's peace, which passes all understanding, we would always worry about tomorrow and what it will bring. Worry and fear are first cousins, and both are an insult to God. They say to God, *"You are not great enough to take care of my every need."* It says to God, *"This is a problem I need to take care of myself, I cannot trust you on this one God. You just sit back and watch me in action. But God, do not go too far, I might need you as a back-up plan, but first, I want to try and handle it on my own."*

The fruit of peace says, *"I will go to God first, I will listen to God's will for my life. Wherever it leads me, I will follow."* The fruit of peace reminds us of the words of David, *"The Lord is my Shepherd, I shall not want." (Ps 23:1, KJV)*

When the Church allows peace to be absent from its membership, egos get in the way and pride takes over. Soon bickering over interpretation of scripture, and solutions to everyday problems lead to schisms, or more commonly called, denominationalism. The Church will only come together as one when we allow God to once again take charge, run the show, inspire the program and lay out the plan. Then love, joy, and peace, God's **passion fruits**, will bring us together in Christian Unity.

----

2)

The second lesson we learn comes from the next category of fruit we find in God's fruit market, **_FRUCTOSE PRODUCING FRUIT._** Read v22b, *"...patience, kindness, goodness." (Gal 5:22, RSV)*

Now *Fructose producing fruits* have natural sugar and are found in sweet fruits such as apples, plums, and grapes. These fruits have a sweet taste and are often stored for long time consumption when they are converted to preserves or dried and canned.

Fructose producing fruits are nature's candy and eating them leaves a sweet taste on our lips and when consumed between meals, they help alleviate our hunger for more fatty and unhealthy snacks. The fructose producing fruits that you will find in God's fruit market are **patience, kindness, and goodness.** These are the qualities that make being a Christian taste sweet to the world. While everybody around us would take up arms, throw in the towel and give up, refuse to be kind to their enemies, God's Spirit is saying no – we must act differently! We must show the sweetness of the Holy Spirit through patience. We must show kindness by turning the other cheek while at the same time, sharing compassion and defusing a volatile situation.

When Paul lists goodness and kindness as two of the fruits of the Spirit, he has something definite in mind. The Galatian Christians were plotting against one another and showing no kindness towards one another. They were devising evil plans to assassinate one another's character. Therefore, when Paul uses the word **goodness** he means to be of moral excellence, upright, to be benevolent and kind.

This was lacking in the community of Galatia. Paul tells them to accept the Spirit in their lives and goodness will automatically come as a result. But this could only happen if they turned away from the works of the flesh. *(Gal 5:19, RSV)* The two are incompatible and contrary by nature. They are vying for control in a Christian's life.

When we accept Jesus the Christ the Spirit allows us to do good. Goodness then becomes a way of life or a goal we try to achieve in our character and through our actions. When we have accomplished this, we can say in the words of King David, *"Surely goodness and mercy shall follow me all the days of my life, and I will dwell in the house of the Lord forever." (Ps 23:6, RSV)*

---

3)

The third and final category in God's fruit market is called **STONE FRUITS.** Read vv 22c-23, *"...faithfulness, meekness, and self-control." (Gal 5:22c-23, RSV)*

A **stone fruit** is defined as *"a fruit with a central stone or hard endocarp, as a peach or plum."* I Peter 2: 4-5 tells us, *"Come to him, to that living stone, rejected by men but in God's sight chosen and precious; and like living stones, be yourselves built into a spiritual house, to be a holy priesthood, to offer spiritual sacrifices acceptable to God through Jesus Christ." (RSV)*

The three **stone fruits** are essential parts of a Christian's character. The first listed here is **faithfulness.** *(Gal 5:22, RSV)* Oftentimes when Paul would leave a community where he founded a Church, some naysayers and Jewish Christians would come to town and challenge Paul's authority and teachings. However, Paul hoped that before he exited a city, he had established and grounded the people so deeply that they would remain faithful to the cause of Christ. This was not the case in Galatia. *(Gal 1:6-9, RSV)*

It seems that the Corinthian and Galatian Churches were easily persuaded when opposing theologies were presented to them. Their status as "babes in Christ" caused them to falter under demonic and heretical teachings. *(Gal 3:1, RSV)* Yet, when Paul challenged them through his letters, the faithful ones were able to take control of the situation and return to the teachings of Jesus, according to Paul. *(Gal 6:1-6, RSV)*

Faithfulness no matter the challenge is a **stone fruit** that grounds the Church when the storms of the secular world try to destroy us or pollute our faith in a risen Christ. Jesus is the stone that cannot be removed. As Christians, our faithfulness comes from our relationship with God and the reading of God's word. If we stay connected to these two anchors, we will be faithful until God calls us home for our reward.

Another stone fruit, *meekness* is also a fructose producing fruit. However, when we think of a person as meek, the qualities that come to mind are quiet, calm, patient, and submissive. These are the qualities of character for Paul that one needs to grasp the true meaning of the gospel of Jesus the Christ. *(Gal 5:24-25, RSV)*

For the gospel message strips us of all vanity, pride, and ego. On the one hand, we are given the highest title *"Sons of God"* because of our faith in a risen Christ.*(Mt 5:9, RSV)* Then on the other hand, without this faith, we are as filthy rags in the eyesight of God because of our past sins. *(Isa 64:6, RSV)* What meekness does is teach us that we have all sinned and fallen short of the glory of God! But because of grace we are justified and made perfect before God. *(Rom 3:23-24, RSV)*

This is the message Paul tries to get across to the Galatian Church. They have fallen out of grace because of Paul's enemies who are teaching them the wrong way. They are teaching obedience to Moses' laws as the only way to salvation.

Paul says NO! There is nothing we can do on our own to merit salvation. It is a gift from God! Only our egos convince us that it is because of something we have done on our own that makes us saved. Only self-righteousness tells us we have somehow earned a seat in heaven. That is why *meekness* is so important. It keeps us humble. It lays out the right frame of mind to receive God's will in our lives. It reminds us of our status in creation and of our relationship to the Creator. Ps 100:3 reminds us, *"Know that the Lord is God! It is he that made us, and we are his; we his people and the sheep of his pasture." (RSV)*

The meek in the Bible were usually poor people. They magnified the Lord with thanksgiving. They praised the name of God. *(Ps 69:30-33, RSV)*

Our final **stone fruit** is **self-control.** This is a tough one. Self-control seems to be a dying characteristic in society today. Everybody seems to think they have a right to their own opinion and behavior choices, despite how it may infringe upon somebody else's rights. Self-control is so necessary both in the Church and the secular world. A lack of self-control is usually a sign of impulsiveness, a sense of entitlement, or superiority over others.

When we exhibit self-control, we allow others to have different opinions, beliefs, and lifestyles that we may not necessarily agree with, but they can live their own lives. Self-control frees us from retribution, retaliation, and unlimited arguments. Self-control says that the Church is open to hearing new and creative ideas. Self-control says that the Church can control its own desires and appetites and when necessary, discipline its own with love and forgiveness. We are the living stones that can be built into a spiritual house and become a priesthood of all believers. *(I Pet 2:5, RSV)*

When the Church practices self-control, we can all come to the table in Christian Unity and celebrate the broken body and the shed blood. For self-control involves tolerance, patience, love and acceptance. When we achieve those gifts, 11 A.M. on Sunday morning will no longer be the most segregated hour of the week.

When Jesus came upon a fig tree that had no fruit, he sentenced it to death. *(Mk 11:12-14, RSV)* The Church was created to share the fruits of the Spirit. If the Church fails in this capacity, Jesus will have the last say. God bless you!

THE LETTER TO THE EPHESIANS

(Disputed)

Acknowledging the Glory of God

THE CHURCH'S RESPONSE TO GOD'S GOODNESS

EPHESIANS 3:20-21, *"Now to him who by the power at work within us is able to do far more abundantly than all that we ask or think, to him be glory in the Church and in Christ Jesus to all generations, forever and ever. AMEN! (RSV)*

INTRODUCTION

The book of Ephesians is a letter written to the Church located in the town of Ephesus. This was a Gentile town that had heard the gospel of Jesus the Christ and accepted the preaching of missionaries who had visited the town to proclaim the new salvation found in Jesus the Christ. The author of Ephesians, whom some scholars say was Paul, writes this letter from prison in order to encourage the new converts in their faith.

Paul does not want them to get discouraged because of his imprisonment. Instead he writes to them in v13, *"So I ask you not to lose heart over what I am suffering for you; which is your glory." (Eph 3:13, RSV)* In other words, because Paul's preaching resulted in their conversion, he was in jail! However, Paul does not see this as a defeat, but an honor. Christ suffered for the same reason – the preaching of God's coming kingdom and the inclusivity of God's love. For Paul this was something to praise God for.

There are three lessons from the Lord that our text will teach us as we listen closely for a word from the Lord. ***TO GOD BE THE GLORY!***

1)

The first lesson we receive from the text is that ***GOD'S BLESSINGS ARE AVAILABLE TO ALL***. Read v16, *"That according to the riches of his glory he may grant you to be strengthened with might through his Spirit in the inner man." (Eph 3:16, RSV)*

Paul reminds the Ephesian Christians of their status in the eyes of God before Christ came. They were not Jews, but Gentiles; not a part of the seed of Abraham or the chosen elect, but strangers who were not included in the original promises of God.

This prior status meant certain death in the eyes of God. They did not know the commandments that were given to Moses on Mt. Sinai. *(Exo 20, RSV)* They were unfamiliar with the cleansing ritual of circumcision or the dietary laws in the book of Leviticus.*(Lev 11;12:3, RSV)* They were ignorant of the sacrifices that one could offer up on the altars of the temple in Jerusalem in order to receive God's forgiveness and absolution. *(Lev 1:4, RSV)* Before they heard the gospel message of salvation, they were in a state of lostness. *(Jn 3:16, RSV)*

Now that has all been changed because of the life and death of Jesus of Nazareth. Paul prays for them. He prays that according to the riches of God's glory they may be strengthened within. The riches of God's glory refer to the many privileges we receive because of our salvation through Christ. One very important privilege is the anointing of the Holy Spirit, which reveals to us the knowledge and peace of God. *(Eph 3:16, RSV)*

This strengthening of the inner Spirit helps us to stand tall in the middle of life's worst tribulations. The Holy Spirit anchors us and keeps us from becoming uprooted when it seems that the world is against us. The Ephesians saw the one who preached the gospel to them with such conviction, now imprisoned, and in the hands of the Roman government. Were they next? Should they denounce publicly all the teachings about a risen Christ that seemed to offend the Roman government? What would happen to them now?

As Christians, we face life's crises every day. Sometimes we want to question our faith in the true and living God. Sometimes we get weak and start considering alternative methods of spirituality. But know that Paul's prayer is still relevant today. We still have access to the riches of God's glory. We have the victory already. *"For he who is in you is greater than he who is in the world."* *(I John 4:4, RSV)* **TO GOD BE THE GLORY!**

---

2)

The second lesson we learn is that ***CHRIST MUST BE ACCEPTED WITH OUR HEARTS FIRST, THEN WITH OUR MINDS.*** Read v17, *"…and that Christ may dwell in your hearts through faith; that you, being rooted and grounded in love." (Eph 3:17, RSV)*

Paul realizes that everything he and others taught the Ephesian Christians may seem like hogwash now that he was in jail. Paul prays that Christ might dwell in their hearts through faith. You notice Paul did not say in their minds or intellect. That is what philosophers taught. For Paul, if you only know Christ with your head, then Christmas is a fairy tale to you and the resurrection is only a rumor. If you only know Christ because you read about him somewhere, then the full impact of what God did for a dying world has not yet penetrated your spiritual psyche and your behavior remains the same. *(Eph 3:17, RSV)*

But when you know Christ through your heart, love fills your being. Love overcomes all temptations and redemption replaces eternal destruction. When you know Christ through your heart and not just with your head, you can get up to testify about how good God has been to you and somebody will feel your testimony, not just hear it. It becomes evident in your walk, in your talk, in your smile, and throughout every aspect of your life.

When we accept Christ in our hearts, only then will faith kick in. What seemed impossible now looks possible through the eyes of faith. That is why Paul wrote, *"I can do all things in him who strengthens me." (Phil 4:13, RSV)* What looked like a mountain, through faith is only a molehill. The power of faith is the greatest power in the world because it is grounded in our love for God. It makes you love your enemies, folk who you know are out to destroy you, you can just smile and leave them in the hands of God. *(Mt 5:10-11, RSV)*

This is the love that Christ showed to the world. Even as he hung on the cross, in pain and humiliation, he too prayed for those who were responsible for his death, *"Father forgive them; for they know not what they do." (Lk 23:34, RSV)*

Paul knew if the Ephesians could receive that kind of love, they would not hate the Roman government for his imprisonment. They could not hate the Jews who did not want to accept them as co-heirs of the promises of God. Instead if they believed in Christ with their whole heart, because of the teaching they received, Christ's love would ground them at their weakest moments. For Paul said, *"…for when I am weak, then I am strong." (II Cor 12:10, RSV)* **TO GOD BE THE GLORY!**

---

3)

The third and final lesson teaches us that ***AFTER WE ACCEPT JESUS CHRIST IN OUR HEARTS, WE MUST THEN LEARN GOD'S WAYS AND WILL FOR OUR LIVES.*** Read vv18-19, *"May have power to comprehend with all the saints, what is the breadth and length and height and depth, and to know the love of Christ which surpasses knowledge, that you may be filled with all the fullness of God." (Eph 3:18-19, RSV)*

The Gentile Christians had a lot to learn about who God is, and what God had to do to insure their salvation. Paul prays that they receive enough power from the Holy Spirit to understand as much as possible what God's will is for all creation. Paul describes the total fullness of God by using the measurements – ***BREADTH, LENGTH, HEIGHT, AND DEPTH*** – to pontificate the vastness of God's being. *(Eph 3:18, RSV)*

When we think about the ***breadth*** of God, we envision a God so wide that his love can embrace all who are willing to receive the gift of eternal live through faith in his Son. God is not narrow. God shows no partiality. *(Acts 10:34, RSV)* Jesus' blood covers all who are willing to surrender to God's grace and mercy.

The ***length*** of God's love references to how long God has already loved us, and how God intends to love us throughout all eternity. The Old Testament reveals the history of God's love for us, which began at Creation and extended unto the book of Revelation, where a new heaven and a new earth will be revealed. *(Rev 21:1, RSV)*

The ***height*** of God's love refers to those who make-up the heavenly courts. They praise God all day long and are obedient to the will of God doing God's bidding between heaven and the earth. *(Isa 6:1-8, RSV)*

The *depth* of God's love reveals the determination and power of God. God sent his only begotten Son into the fiery pits of hades just to make sure all who belong to the fold would be saved. *(Acts 2:31; Eph 4:8-10; I Pet 3:18-20, RSV)* Now that is love! The Psalmist wrote, *"Whither shall I go from thy Spirit?... If I ascend to the heaven, thou art there! If I make my bed in Sheol, thou art there!" (Ps 139:7-8, RSV)*

This is the fullness of God's glory. Whatever it takes to bring us back into a right relationship with God, God has already done it. Once the Ephesian Church learns of this, their faith and love in God will be steadfast, unmovable, and together with all the saints, and fellow believers, God will be praised! *(I Pet 3:d, RSV)* **TO GOD BE THE GLORY!**

Paul ends his prayer with a benediction. Even as he sits in a prison cell, Paul can still feel the glory of God all around him. So he concludes his prayer with these words of praise and thanksgiving, *"Now to him who by the power at work within us is able to do far more abundantly than all that we can ask or think, to him be glory in the Church and in Christ Jesus, to all generations forever and ever. AMEN! (Eph 3:20-21, RSV)*

It is God who works through us – to **God be the glory!** It is God who accomplishes miracles beyond our capacity to imagine – to **God be the glory**! It is God working through the Church to bring sinners back to the fold – to **God be the glory**! It was God who took on flesh, born of a virgin woman, healed the sick, fed the hungry, gave sight to the blind, raised the dead – and one day saved you and me from eternal death. **TO GOD BE THE GLORY FOR THE THINGS HE HAS DONE TO RECONCILE THE WORLD TO HIMSELF** in the past, continues to do in the present, and will do in the future for all those generations who will not know the Lord Jesus Christ in the pardoning of their sins. **TO GOD BE THE GLORY! AMEN!**

THE LETTER TO THE PHILIPPIANS

(Undisputed)

Right Thinking Leads to Right Actions

WHAT ARE YOU THINKING ABOUT?

PHILIPPIANS 4:1-9, *"Finally brethren, whatever is true, whatever is honorable, whatever is just, whatever is pure, whatever is lovely, whatever is gracious, if there is any excellence, if there is anything worthy of praise, think about these things. What you have learned and received and heard and seen in me, do; and the God of peace will be with you." (RSV)*

INTRODUCTION

Paul started the Church in the city of Philippi, named after King Philip of Macedonia. He was also the father of Alexander the Great. Philippi was a major link between the east and the west, traveling west from Rome and going east to Byzantine *(the country of Turkey today)*. We find the report of Paul's founding this Church in Acts 16:6-40, RSV.

Paul visited the Church 2-3 times after its organization and this Church became Paul's closest and most supportive system throughout his many trials and tribulations, even when he was in prison. *(Phil 1:3-5, RSV)*

Paul writes this letter to the Philippians for 4 reasons. *First,* he wanted to communicate with them that Epaphroditius, their colleague and Paul's fellow worker in Christ, was coming back home to Philippi. This meant he could carry this letter with them, since there was no post office back then. *(Phil 2:25-26, RSV) Secondly,* because now he is in prison and they are concerned about his wellbeing. *Thirdly,* the Church was facing some internal problems – some members were not getting along (imagine that!) causing division and discord. It just so happens they were two women – Eurodia and Syntyche.*(Phil 4:1-3, RSV)* Then *fourthly* Paul writes this letter because he knew that they were facing persecutions on the outside, from the same people who were responsible for him being in jail. *(Phil 1:30, RSV)*

Yet through all the problems that existed in Philippi, and within the Philippian Church, Paul wanted them to have peace of mind. For Paul knew that without peace of mind, the heart and the body will begin to deteriorate, and the soul will lose its fight against outside demonic forces. *(Phil 4:8-9, RSV)*

Then, the question asked this morning is, *"What are you thinking about?"* What thoughts go through your mind 24/7? Are your thoughts good, keeping you spiritually and mentally healthy? Or are they evil, perverted, tainted, causing permanent damage to your heart and soul? Remember, whatever you think in your heart will determine your behavior. *(Mt 9:4, RSV)* Therefore, let us think about these words in our text as we ponder together the lessons Paul want us to learn.

---

1)

If we look at our text, we see that Paul wants us to learn that **_PEACE OF MIND COMES WITH THE JOY OF THE LORD._** Read v4 *"Rejoice in the Lord always; again I will say, rejoice." (Phil 4:4, RSV)*

Paul has been through a great deal in his life. Now as he comes to the end of his race, he reflects back on everything he has lived through: persecutions of Christians for the Pharisees *(Acts 9, RSV)*; struck down by the light of the resurrected Jesus on the road to Damascus *(Acts 9:4, RSV)*; employed as the Apostle to the Gentiles *(Acts 9:15, RSV)*; organized Churches as he traveled through Asia Minor which included the cities of Corinth, Galatia, Thessalonica, Ephesus; summoned to Macedonia then Greece and backtracking to Jerusalem to provide financial support to the victims of famine and drought; preaching and teaching the gospel message wherever he went, whatever the circumstances. *(Acts 26:19-23, RSV)*

Paul was telling a dying world that Jesus died and arose so that they can find salvation through Jesus and be reconciled back to the Father. Paul was shipwrecked, beaten and left for dead, run out of town, hungry at times, full at times, sometimes cold, sometimes hot. He was imprisoned at least 3 times that we know of! *(Phil 4:11-12; Acts 22:19; 2 Cor 6:5, RSV)*

Yet he learned to be content no matter what his circumstances. He had no regrets. It was all worth it. He counted it all as joy! Now he has a crown of glory awaiting him in Heaven. *(2 Tim 4:8, RSV)*

Paul knew firsthand that serving Jesus was no bed of roses. But the reward is not down here. He will get his reward on judgment day. That is what makes us smile and rejoice through it all. The Gospel artist Kirk Franklin sings a song called "Smile." The message in the song is that whatever you are going through just smile. Not because it feels good, but because we know God is with us, and that God is able to see us through.

Therefore, let us rejoice! Think about God's goodness in your life. Think about what God has already brought you through. What are you thinking about? Are they good thoughts? Are they positive thoughts? How and what you think about determines your destiny in life.

---

2)

After Paul reminds the Philippian Church to hold onto their joy, his next words of advice to help them sustain peace of mind is **_TRUST IN THE LORD AND PRAY!_** Read v6, *"Have no anxiety about anything, but in everything by prayer and supplication with thanksgiving let your requests be made known to God." (Phil 4:6, RSV)*

Paul now offers prayer and trust in God as the solution to worry. Paul knows they are worried about him and how long he will be in prison or if he will be released this time. They sent him writing supplies, blankets, money and food. Whatever Paul needed to experience physical comfort while he was in prison, they were eager to provide. They loved Paul, and never strayed away from his teachings. *(Phil 4:18, RSV)*

However, Paul has learned of the difficulties that the Philippian Church is facing while he is incarcerated. There are conflicts both within and without. Paul knew that a divided house could not stand. First things first! Paul tells the two sources of conflict – Eurodia and Syntyche – to get it together! Stop fighting! Stop jockeying for position and power! Instead, work together for the good of the whole Church, and not just for your own personal gain. Trust in the Lord and pray for one another. *(Phil 4:2-3, RSV)*

Paul knew if the Church was going to survive outside attacks, they needed to be unified and on one accord, agreeing in the Holy Spirit. Paul tells them to pray. These two women needed to come together before the Church and allow the whole congregation to pray for and with them. The Church is not to worry for that shows a lack of trust in God, and in the gospel message they have learned from Paul.

Paul does not want them to think about anything that would steal their joy, or cause worry to infiltrate their souls and minds. What about us today? What are you thinking about? What is hindering you from giving your full attention to God? What are you thinking about? Work? Play? Family? Bills? Pain? Relationships?

Paul tells us to pray and do not worry. *But in everything by prayer and supplication with thanksgiving, let your requests be made known to God."* *(Phil 4:6, RSV)* What does worrying do? How does worrying help alleviate the situation? It does not, it only gives you stress which leads to high cholesterol, high blood pressure, overeating, cancer. It is a tool of the devil to destroy our bodies, our relationships and even our jobs! *(Jn 10:10, RSV)*

As believers, we have been with Jesus long enough to know that through all our trials and tribulations, we can depend upon God's word. Paul spoke these words from his own experiences of the good, the bad, and the ugly of being a witness for Jesus. Yet he never faltered or gave up. For Paul *"…to live is Christ and to die was gain."* *(Philippians 1:21, RSV)*

Just pray about it. James says the prayer of the righteous is powerful and effective. *(James 5:16c, RSV)* Maybe you are afraid to pray because you are not living a holy and righteous life. God knows your heart and your situation. Pray anyhow! Repent first and ask for forgiveness. God does hear a repented sinner's prayer! *(Rom 10:9-10, RSV)* So do not worry, be happy! For even though all around you is collapsing, know that then Jesus is your hope and stay. Therefore, stand on the solid rock of Jesus our Lord and Savior. What are you thinking about?

---

3)

Our final lesson lists the very things that we ought to think about that will under gird and guard our peace of mind. Paul's advice to the Philippian Church and to us is that ***PEACE***

OF MIND COMES THROUGH RIGHT THINKING AND RIGHT ACTION. Read vv8-9, *"Finally brethren, whatever is true, whatever is honorable, whatever is just, whatever is pure, whatever is lovely, whatever is gracious, if there is any excellence and if there is anything worthy of praise, think about these things." (Phil 4:8-9, RSV)*

Paul reminds the Church that there is a connection between what we think and how we act. He has encouraged them to keep their joy by focusing on what God has already done for them through Christ. He has provided them with a means to protect their joy by encouraging them to stay prayed up and trust God will work it out. Now Paul wants them to intentionally place their focus on only the positive, avoiding all negative thoughts and influences whenever possible. *(Phil 4:8, RSV)*

Paul knows that this involves mental and spiritual fortitude. For evil thoughts come at us all the time, disrupting our peace of mind, trying to steal our joy. That is what happened to Eve in the Garden of Eden. An evil thought in the form of a serpent, came to her and told her that God was a liar; and she believed him! *(Gen 3:1-7, RSV)* And ladies, we have been paying for her mistake ever since.

The busyness of life keeps us from setting aside time to read the Bible, and special prayer time so we grow weak spiritually, making us prime targets and susceptible to the wiles of the devil. *(Eph 6:11, RSV)*

Yet when we pray and trust in God, *"We are more than conquerors through him who loved us." (Romans 8:37, RSV)* Yes, we can control our thinking! How? - By not allowing worldly thoughts to linger in our minds. Think instead on whatever is true, not gossip. Think instead on whatever is honorable, lifting one another up. Think instead on whatever is just and stand up for the right things. Think instead on whatever is pure, and avoid things that pollute your mind, body and soul. *(Phil 4:8, RSV)* Think instead on whatever is pleasing, for without faith it is impossible to please God. *(Heb 11:6, RSV)* Think instead on that which is excellent and worthy of praise, Jesus Christ our King!

Church, when you think about Jesus, it makes you want to act like Jesus, love like Jesus, forgive like Jesus, trust in God like Jesus did while hanging on a cross between two thieves. What are you thinking about that makes you act the way you do? God bless you!

THE LETTER TO THE COLOSSIANS

(Disputed)

Is There Order In The House?

KEEPING ORDER IN GOD'S HOUSE

COLOSSIANS 3:17-19, *"And whatever you do, in word or deed, do everything in the name of the Lord Jesus, giving thanks to God the Father through him. Wives, be subject to your husbands, as is fitting in the Lord. Husbands, love your wives, and do not be harsh with them… Whatever your task, work heartily, as serving the Lord and not men, knowing that from the Lord you will receive the inheritance as your reward; you are serving the Lord Christ! (RSV)*

INTRODUCTION

It is believed by most scholars, that Paul wrote the letter to the Colossians, while he was in prison in Rome. Paul himself had never visited Colossae, but he sent his colleague in the ministry, Epaphras, and he was successful at starting a congregation through the preaching of the gospel of Jesus the Christ. Colossae was not an important city in and of itself, and it was situated on the river. *(Col 1:4-8, RSV)*

Epaphras brought reports of his work in Colossae to Paul. He would share the good news, as well as the bad news. This letter is a response to some very disturbing news from Epaphras. This news revealed to Paul the problem of false preachers in Colossae, who were distorting the gospel message by combining some pagan rituals and practices with a philosophy of angelic mediators. They claimed these angelic mediators had a higher knowledge than Christ, and that one could obtain this knowledge through a strict disciplined lifestyle, which brought them in sync with these angelic beings. *(Col 2:18, RSV)* Paul writes this letter to confirm the truth of the gospel as preached by Epaphras and to expose the false philosophy of his enemies. *(Col 2:8, RSV)*

Now these verses are very infamous in the Christian Church because of phrases like, *"wives be subject to your husbands"; "husbands love your wives";* and *"children obey your parents in everything."* *(Col 3:18-20, RSV)* But unfortunately, for many years, these seemingly oppressive verses have been taken out of context and used to argue and misconstrue the proper order in a relationship between husbands/wives, father/children, and children/parents.

Let us therefore examine these verses more closely and listen for a lesson that will bless our lives as we attempt to keep order in God's House.

1)

The first lesson we learn from our text regarding keeping order in God's house is that ***SERVING OTHERS IS TO BE LIKE CHRIST.*** Read v18, *"Wives be subject to your husbands, as is fitting in the Lord." (Col 3:18, RSV)*

Paul's letter to the Colossians is the first and only time he deals with these areas of social life – wives/husbands, children/father, and slaves/masters. For you see everyone was expecting a rapid return of Christ. Christians sold all that they had and pooled their resources, expecting the kingdom to descend upon them at any moment. *(Acts 2:44-46, RSV)* Well, after several decades passed, and Jesus had not yet returned, an order of life needed to be established so people would know what their role was, and their place in this pre-kingdom come status.

Now the Greeks already had a social order in place in Colossae. So, Paul just adopted the social order of that community and adds a slightly different flavor to it. You see the Greek social order was designed to oppress, dominate, manipulate, and degrade. But Paul tells wives that serving your husbands is not an oppressive status, it is not an inferior state of being, but rather it is equal to the submission Jesus surrendered to the Father, when he agreed to take on flesh and come on earth. It is all in how you look at it. *(Col 3:18, RSV)*

Paul reminds them that this same submission Jesus experienced in life and on the cross, but Jesus reclaimed his royal status on the third day. Paul teaches the wives that submission in Jesus today leads to salvation and victory over this life later. *(Col 3:24, RSV)*

The Greek word for ***"submit"*** *"huotasso"* is not in the active voice – which means it is not mandatory, nor is it in the passive voice, which means someone has the right to do it to you despite your objection. No! The word is in the middle voice, which means that as wives we choose to submit ourselves, we make the choice, it is a voluntary action, not a command written in stone. Jesus was not forced to take on flesh. Jesus chose to be born of a virgin and die for our sins.

In other words, in that same way we can choose to be submissive. Therefore, the verb does in no way imply our inferiority. It only offers a role, a place, if appropriate, for us so that we can help keep order in God's House. Then Paul reminds us that if we choose to do so, it is fitting, pleasing, and in harmony with the will of God. There is no shame attached to it.

2)

The second lesson we learn from this text about keeping order in God's house is that ***THE LOVE OF CHRIST UNDERGIRDS THE RELATIONSHIP BETWEEN HUSBAND AND WIFE.*** Read v19, *"Husbands, love your wives, and do not be harsh with them." (Col 3:19, RSV)*

The exhortation to submit voluntarily to the husband is balanced with the instruction to husbands to love their wives. In both cases the admonition is an appeal to free and responsible persons that can heed the suggestion voluntarily, never by breaking down the human will, or oppressing the other. The motivation for Paul is the love of Christ. For only what you do for Christ will sustain the relationship. *(Col 3:14, RSV)*

Now the husband's love is not simply a matter of affectionate feelings or intimacy. Rather, it involves the husband's increasing care and loving service towards his wife's entire wellbeing. Husbands are to love wives as Christ loves the Church. *(Eph 5:25, RSV)* This is a love that is sacrificial, that has no regard for self, and is defined by the actions of Jesus. When Paul thinks about love, he is referring to I Corinthians 13, his love letter to the Church in Corinth.

If husbands love their wives in this manner, then they will have no need to play macho, or mistreat her, thinking that is how a real man treats his wife. All areas of married life will be characterized by this self-giving love and forgiveness. That was the way it was originally meant to be before Adam and Eve fell from grace. *(Gen 2:24, RSV)*

Then Paul encourages husbands not to be harsh with their wives. *(Col 3:19, RSV)* She may burn a meal or two, but love her anyhow. She may get irritable and tired from work outside the home and must work some more when she gets home but love her the same. Be patient through PMS, pregnancy, hot flashes and menopause because that is the life cycle of a woman. She may get jealous or acknowledge the presence of a *"headache"* when you are in a romantic mood but love her through it all!

Remember, Christ loves you in all your faults and shortcomings. Remember, God forgives you when you miss the mark. For love covers a multitude of sins. *(I Peter 4:8, RSV)* In God's House you are given the role of the spiritual leader. Yet you are not to hold it over your spouse's head. This is your place in the pre-kingdom come order.

---

3)

The third and final lesson in this text states that **_GOD'S ORDER LEADS TO AN ETERNAL REWARD._** Read v24, *"Knowing that from the Lord you will receive the inheritance as your reward; you are serving the Lord Christ."* *(Col 3:24, RSV)*

Paul continues to set the order in God's House. He tells the little children – **tekna** – to obey their parents in everything. The word *"obey"* is in the active voice, which means it is a command and the children have no choice. Then Paul begins to describe the role of the father in relationship to the children. He is instructed to love them, not provoke them or criticize them to the point where they are discouraged and suffer from low self-esteem. *(Col 3:21, RSV)* Be the best positive role model you can be but put Christ first as the pioneer and perfecter of our faith. *(Heb 12:2, RSV)*

Then finally Paul addresses the category of *"slave and master,"* which today would be equivalent to boss and employee. Paul tells us not to work only when we think the boss is watching because we are not working for any human boss, but for the Master of the Sea, and the Creator of the Universe. *(Col 3:23-24, RSV)* We are to work as if God's name is on our paycheck! The earthly paycheck is only temporal and will soon be spent. But the heavenly paycheck will reap benefits throughout eternity.

We are working for that final reward. We want to receive our eternal reward, to see our names in the Book of Life. *(Rev 3:5, RSV)* We want to walk into the pearly gates and right into the mansion that Jesus has prepared for us. Paul emphasizes that it is never about what we get in return down here. It is never about how big the Church is, the congregation, the car, the house, the paycheck, how well we are dressed, or how much education we have.

All that matters in the end is how well did we keep order in God's House? How well did we work with one another? How deeply did we love each other? How forgiving were we of each other's faults?

The main purpose for keeping order in God's House is to receive the reward of inheritance. The reward comes first in serving the Lord Jesus Christ, according to the order in the Scriptures. If we get the order right down here, our reward and inheritance will be confirmed. Therefore, keeping order in God's House requires 3 things: 1) serving others to be like Christ, 2) allowing love to undergird our relationship between husband and wife, and 3) if we are obedient, keeping order in God's House leads to our eternal reward, everlasting life! God bless you!

THE FIRST LETTER TO THE THESSALONIANS

(Undisputed)

*Prayer is the Key to the Kingdom, but
Our Faith Unlocks the Door*

IT IS PRAYING TIME!

I THESSALONIANS 5:16-18, *Rejoice always, pray constantly, give thanks in all circumstances; for this is the will of God in Christ Jesus for you." (RSV)*

INTRODUCTION

Paul, Silas, and Timothy are the 3 missionaries who first brought the gospel to Thessalonica and planted the Church there. Shortly after their arrival, they met with much conflict, tribulation and attacks. They left Thessalonica in order to protect the converts there from further harassment from the authorities. *(I Th 2:16, RSV)* Just a few weeks later, Paul writes this letter to see how they are doing as new believers and *"babes in Christ." (I Cor 3:1, RSV)*

Paul's letter to the Thessalonians is the first and earliest of all his letters. It was written less than 20 years after the ascension of Christ. Now in our text we read these words, *"Rejoice always, pray constantly, give thanks in all circumstances." (I Th 5:16, RSV)* These three short phrases represent a theological and biblical trilogy for Paul – Rejoice – pray- give thanks. These 3 words are the foundation of Paul's efforts to evangelize and bring people to Christ.

If we read and study them, we will discover that they are still words of advice to all Christians today. Why rejoice? - Because our joy is a testimony to the world that we believe God is in control. Why pray without ceasing? - Because prayer is our major avenue of communication to God, and the Holy Trinity. Why give thanks? - Because gratitude helps us keep life in perspective and helps us to be content in our present situations knowing all the time that we are in God's care.

Let us now discuss the theological trilogy and focus only on the power of prayer in the life of the believer.

---

1)

The first lesson we learn about prayer is that ***PRAYER SERVES AS A PRESERVATIVE FOR OUR SOULS. (RSV)*** Read v2, *"For you yourselves know well that the day of the Lord will come like a thief in the night." (I Th 5:2, RSV)*

Paul writes these words because he is concerned about his sudden departure from Thessalonica. He was not there long enough to teach the new converts everything they needed to know in order to withstand the attacks of the authorities and non-believers. But Paul learns later after he sent Timothy back to check on the new converts, that what he had taught them stuck, took root. *(I Th 3:1-3, RSV)* They were able to grow from the seeds that Paul had planted in the short time he was with them.

Timothy reported they were doing just fine! They were growing in the love and knowledge of Jesus the Christ. They were keeping close and careful watch for the return of Christ. *(I Th 3:6-10, RSV)*

Prayer is what preserves us in our wait for Christ's return. It gives us the patience and discipline we need to wait month after month, and year after year, praying for God's kingdom to come quickly. Prayer keeps our hope alive so that we do not sleep in our faith and do not grow weary in well doing.*(Ga 6:9, RSV)* For when we pray, power from heaven is released and our spiritual batteries get recharged.

When life has thrown everything at us, and we are experiencing great trials and tribulations, it is a strong and fervent prayer life that steadies our souls and reminds us that this is not all there is, that we are just pilgrims traveling through this barren land. We believe that one day Jesus is coming back, and he will be looking for a Church without a spot or wrinkle. *(Eph 5:27, RSV) Therefore*, we must keep our eyes on the prize and be vigilant in our prayer life. *(Phil 3:14, RSV)*

---

2)

The second lesson we learn about prayer is that ***PRAYER AFFECTS OUR RELATIONSHIP WITH GOD AND OUR NEIGHBOR***. Read v15, "*See that none of you repays evil for evil, but always seek to do good to one another and to all.*" *(I Th 5:15, RSV)*

The Thessalonian Christians were living in a very difficult situation. The Jewish leaders wanted their testimonies to cease. The Roman authorities were charging them with treason because of their claim that Jesus was their Lord and King. The pagans had idol gods everywhere, a consistent threat of their old ways of doing religion. They were in a minority and an unpopular one at that! For these same people ran Paul, Silas and Timothy out of town! *(I Th 2:2, RSV)*

Yet Paul's advice to them is to pray without ceasing. What does that mean? The renown New Testament scholar, F.F. Bruce, says the following about praying without ceasing: "*To pray without ceasing does not mean that every other activity must be dropped for the sake of prayer, but that every activity must be carried on in a spirit of prayer which is the spontaneous outcome of a sense of God's presence.*" *(F.F. Bruce. I & 2 Thessalonians. WBC, Waco, Texas; Word Pub. 1982, p 113)*

In other words, our minds ought to always be in sync with God's will for us through constant communication with God. Prayer means to be in the presence, the aura, and the majesty of God. It requires a closeness that comes from our efforts to live a holy life and our salvation through Jesus the Christ.

Once we have established and secured our relationship with God, how we pray and what we pray for then affects our neighbor, for God does answer prayer! So be careful what you pray about. *"See that none of you repays evil for evil, but always seek to do good to one another and to all."(I Th 5:15, RSV)* Therefore we must pray for our enemies, for those who despitefully use us and betray us.

I know being human, it is hard to pray for one's enemies. Yet, that is exactly what Paul says we must do! Pray not for their destruction, but for their deliverance from evil and their salvation. Prayer is both vertical and horizontal. How can I say I love God who I have never seen, and hate my neighbor who I deal with every day? *(I Jn 4:20, RSV)*

Prayer keeps our hearts on the path of love. That is why we must do it without ceasing. For Satan will try to convince us to retaliate against every attack, but through prayer we find courage and strength to turn the other cheek. This is our peace. *"For vengeance is mine, I will repay, says the Lord!" (Romans 12:19, RSV)* How you pray does affect other people. Therefore, let us always seek to do the good.

---

3)

The third lesson on prayer from this text is ***WE PRAY BECAUSE IT IS THE WILL OF GOD.*** Read vv16-18, *"Rejoice always, pray constantly, give thanks in all circumstances for this is the will of God in Christ Jesus for you." (I Th 5:16-18, RSV)*

Paul's trilogy – ***rejoice, pray without ceasing, and give thanks*** – is the winning combination for our Christian journey to be successfully completed. That is why Paul tells the Thessalonians to do so. But he also tells them to do these 3 things because it is the will of God in Christ Jesus for you. For these are the words that Jesus often taught his audience and his disciples. REJOICE! PRAY! GIVE THANKS! *(Mt 5:12; 6:9; 15:36)* If we practice these 3 things alone, we will be too busy to participate in evil and take part in strategies to hurt others.

Our relationship with God will be secure and our faith will empower us to do great things. You see when we pray without ceasing the line to God is always open for advice, consultation, responses, dialogue and information. We will make better choices, avoid mistakes, and find wisdom for the journey.

Therefore, let us continue to pray as the Lord taught us to pray. Not with malice in our hearts. Not going to God with a long list of *"wants."* Rather let us pray without ceasing for the coming kingdom, for our families, for our schools, for our country and political leaders, for our world, and for the next generation. For it is praying time!

THE SECOND LETTER TO THE THESSALONIANS

(Disputed)

Here Comes The Judge!

HOLD ON: JUDGMENT DAY IS COMING!

2 THESSALONIANS 1:3-12, *"We are bound to give thanks to God always for you, brethren, as it is fitting, because your faith is growing abundantly and the love of every one of you for one another is increasing. Therefore, we ourselves boast of you in the churches of God for your steadfastness and faith in all your persecutions and the afflictions which you are enduring." (RSV)*

INTRODUCTION

Thessalonica is the capital city of Macedonia. Tradition credits the Apostle Paul as the author of both 1 and 2 Thessalonians. Paul writes this letter to encourage the believers not to veer from the Gospel truth or the traditions they received from his teachings.

Paul is thankful for the loyalty and commitment shown by the believers in Thessalonica as well as their faith and steadfastness. Even in the middle of opposition and suffering, they have not faltered. Their faith and love for one another is well known and admired throughout the Christian movement. *(II Th 1:3, RSV)*

Paul wants them to know that their sufferings are not in vain for God is watching and waiting until the opportune time when justice and vengeance will be released upon the world. The Church suffers now to bring about God's new order. Their endurance is an indication that they are God's elect, God's chosen ones who at the end of time will be vindicated and embraced into the glory of God the Father, God the Son and God the Holy Spirit for all eternity. *(II Th 2:13-14, RSV)*

Let us now listen to the words of Paul as he encourages us to hold on because Judgment Day is coming!

1)

The first lesson we learn from Paul's second letter to the Thessalonians is that ***FOLLOWING JESUS IS NOT EASY!*** Read v4, *"Therefore we ourselves boast of you in the Churches of God for your steadfastness and faith in all your persecutions and in the afflictions which you are enduring." (II Th 1:4, RSV)*

This is the first of 3 thanksgivings Paul offers in this letter. Verse 4 highlights the Thessalonian Church's steadfastness. Paul boasts about their behavior in the face of danger and constant threats to their lives. Paul recognized that following Christ in a hostile environment is not easy, especially when it is in direct opposition to other philosophical and religious beliefs of their day and their culturally diverse city. *(II Th 1:4, RSV)*

The teachings and traditions they received from Paul were both Jewish and Christian in nature. Although Paul acknowledged on several occasions that the law could not save you, there were parts of the law that promoted a behavior in sync with the teachings of Christ, the Apostles, and Paul. For example: *The Golden Rule, the 10 Commandments, loving your neighbor, loving your enemies, praying for those who abuse you, giving to the poor, widow and orphan.* (Matt 7:12, Exo 20, Mk 12:31, Zech 7:10, RSV)

These tenets of both the Old and New Testament described a lifestyle and daily practice that was contrary to what these Gentiles knew and experienced before they became Christians. Many gave their lives to Christ thinking it was a short-term commitment because he was coming back soon! But now at least 30 years have passed.

Some even started spreading the false rumor that Christ had returned, and they got left behind! Many sold all they had and were now dependent on others for provisions as they awaited the second coming of Christ, the *Parousia*. Yet they continued to worship God and recognize Jesus as their Lord and Savior. Little did they know, that because of their faith, the kind of backlash they would face. *(II Th 1:4, RSV)*

Now during the Apostolic Period, followers of Christ were persecuted, ostracized, imprisoned, threatened, for no other reason than they served a risen Savior, and his name was Jesus. They quickly learned that following Jesus' teachings was not easy! *(Acts 8:58, RSV)*

When we look at the history of America, history records that this country was started on Christian morals and teachings under the guise of religious freedom. But as we all know that was not the case. Men of ill repute, convicts, the uneducated, were paid to work on ships and given freedom if they left their own countries to venture out on this new world discovery.

However, the Native Americans who first owned this land would tell a different version of our history. They were murdered and forced off their land. Then Africans were brought here in the bottom of ships where many died from disease or jumped overboard to avoid slavery.

Then they taught the slaves about Christianity, with their tainted version, only reading from the New Testament book of Philemon. Paul wrote this letter to encourage a slave master to receive his runaway slave back as a brother in Christ, not as a slave! It was not meant to reinforce their positions on slavery. It was not meant to prove that God mandated slavery, based solely on the color of one's skin. *(I Tim 6:1-2; Philem1:10-14, RSV)*

So now we follow Jesus and worship God in our own unique way and have been for 400 years and counting. We know what the Bible really says. We know how we ought to be treated. We learned the lessons of the 10 Commandments. We learned the lessons of the Golden Rule and the summary of the Law. Now we are followers of the Lamb of God, who takes away the sins of the world. Yet, it still has not been easy. We marched peacefully, trying to live like Jesus.

However, we were met with obstacles of every kind and unjustly targeted and thrown into prison. Yes, peoples of color have suffered greatly in this country because of the color of their skin or the slant of their eyes, when all we wanted to do was breathe, and be accepted as the Americans we were born here to be.

It has been our faith in a risen Savior, in a just God, in a comforting Holy Spirit that has kept people of color in the Church. It is not easy following Jesus today with a decline in church attendance. Many millennials have chosen a different path or expression of spirituality, one different from their parents and grandparents.

It is not easy, turning the other cheek and smiling in the face of those who hate you just because of the color of your skin. It is not easy! But Jesus never promised us an easy go of it. Jesus said, *"If the world hates you, know that it has hated me before it hated you."* *(Jn 15:18, RSV)* Jesus said to his disciples, *"If any man would come after me, let him deny himself and take up his cross and follow me."* *(Mt 16:24, RSV)* Jesus did not say this because it is easy, but because in the end we can trade our crosses for our crowns. Eleven of Jesus' original disciples died horrible and violent deaths. Only John, the beloved disciple, lived out his life.

As believers we know that following Jesus was never meant to be easy or everybody could do it. Only those who God called, sanctified, and justified have the steadfastness and faith to hold out until we see our Savior face to face. Hold on, Judgment Day is coming!

---

2)

The next lesson we learn from Paul's second letter to the Thessalonians is that **_GOD'S JUDGMENT IS RIGHTEOUS!_** Read vv5-6, *"This is evidence of the righteous judgment of God, that you may be made worthy of the kingdom of God, for which you are suffering – since indeed God deems it just to repay with affliction those who afflict you."(II Th 1:5-6, RSV)*

In these verses, Paul presents a commentary on God's justice to contextualize the Church's suffering. The Church in Thessalonica was undergoing severe persecutions and affliction at the time of this letter. Some of the converted Jews and pious Gentiles ran Paul out of town on his first visit! So much animosity came against Paul, that he was unable to return to that city. Paul sent his trusted disciple Timothy in his stead to calm down the rebellion and speak truth to those in power. *(I Th 3:1-3, RSV)*

Much time passed and Jesus had not yet returned in the time frame that Paul thought he would. Twenty-forty years now have elapsed and believers were leaving the Church in search, perhaps of an *easier* religion to follow. However, they did not leave quietly nor did those in the community allow the Christian Church to co-exist among other belief systems.

Perhaps it was the Church's refusal to participate in war, or maybe because they refused to eat the meat offered to idol gods. They absented themselves from riotous living and festival days that honored and worshiped the Roman Emperor, as well as idol statues. They were viewed as different and nobody likes *different!* Fit in, go with the flow, or suffer the consequences.

They chose to suffer the consequences and were persecuted for what they believed. *(I Cor 8:7-11, RSV)*

Yet, they were not deterred. They were not dismayed. They were not complaining. Instead they were faithful and loving towards one another so much so that it became the reputation of the Church! What is your Church's reputation in the community? Paul boasted of their reputation and encouraged them to hold on, Judgment Day is coming.

Now the reason Paul was able to encourage them is because Paul knew that God is a righteous Judge. Paul knew, from his experience on the road to Damascus to arrest and imprison Christians, Jesus could have struck him down dead. But instead, Jesus called him to be an apostle to the Gentiles, non-Jews, for the purpose of building up his kingdom on earth. *(Acts 9, RSV)*

Because the Jews had rejected Jesus, this opened the door for all nations to now receive the blessings of Abraham and become heirs in the family of God. Paul tells them their sacrifices are not for naught. Their afflictions are badges of honor. God sees their afflictions as he did the Hebrews in Egyptian slavery, and when God gets ready to move you better watch out! Just ask Pharaoh and his army who were unsuccessful at retrieving the released slaves. *(Exo 12:31; 14:27-28, RSV)*

God will take vengeance against those who cause our affliction. We need not raise a finger. We need only stay in the lane of righteousness, no matter how provoked we are. No matter how tempted we are to fight back, *"God is our refuge and strength, a very present help in trouble."* *(Ps 46:1, RSV)*

Our resistance to evil will make us worthy of the kingdom of God. When God deals with our enemies, our haters, it will be their just reward for God's judgment is righteous. Hold on, Judgment Day is coming!

---

3)

The third lesson we learn from Paul's second letter to the Thessalonian Church is that **_OUR RELIEF IS IN JESUS._** Read vv7-8, *"and to grant rest with us to you who are afflicted, when the Lord Jesus is revealed from heaven with his mighty angels in flaming fire, inflicting vengeance upon those who do not know God, and upon those who do not obey the gospel of our Lord Jesus."* *(II Th 1:7-8, RSV)*

Belief in the gospel is what distinguishes in the present time, the oppressed from the oppressors, and in the future, the elect from the condemned. Paul reassures the Thessalonians that there will be pay back for those who not only afflict and persecute them now, but Paul and his associates as well. This force will be extraordinary because this will all take place *"when the Lord Jesus is revealed from heaven with his mighty angels in flaming fire."* *(II Th 1:8, RSV)*

In other words, Jesus is not coming back as the Savior. That ship has already sailed. Now Jesus is returning as the Judge of all creation. There will be no negotiations. There will be no purgatory or waiting room so you can reconsider not believing in Jesus. *(II Th 1:8, RSV)*

No, no! Your time is up! Judgment Day is here! Jesus is coming armed with his mighty angels who will do his bidding. They will do the separating - the goats from the sheep, the hireling from the Shepherd, the wicked from the righteous, the believers from the non-believers. We read in Mt 13:41-42, *"The Son of Man will send his angels, and they will gather out of his kingdom all causes of sin and all evil-doers, and throw them into the furnace of fire..."* *(RSV)* The angels are coming with a vengeance against those who do not know God and those who refuse to obey the gospel of our Lord Jesus.

Paul tells the Thessalonians and you and I, that if we believe the gospel message that Jesus taught, we are in the clear. If we believe this gospel, then our names are written in the book of life. *(Rev 3:5, RSV)* If we believe this gospel, that *"...God so loved the world that he gave his only Son and that whosoever believes in him should not perish, but have eternal life,"* then Jesus is our relief! *(Jn 3:16, RSV)* There is no relief without faith in Jesus and his mission.

So, stand firm Church! Remain faithful! Do not give up under pressure! For suffering leads to endurance and endurance leads to retribution and retribution leads to glorification, and it is all a part of God's redemptive plan. *(Rom 5:3-5; II Th 1:5, RSV)* Hold on because Judgment Day is coming! God bless you.

THE PASTORAL
EPISTLES

THE FIRST LETTER TO TIMOTHY

(Disputed)

Saved By Grace; Vindicated Through Mercy

THANK GOD FOR MERCY!

I TIMOTHY 1:12-17, *"I thank him who has given me strength for this, Christ Jesus our Lord, because he judged me faithful and appointing me to his service, though even though I formerly blasphemed, and persecuted, and insulted him; but I received mercy because I had acted ignorantly in unbelief, and the grace of our Lord overflowed for me with the faith and love that are in Christ Jesus. The saying is sure and worthy of full acceptance, that Christ Jesus came into the world to save sinners. And I am the foremost of sinners. But I received mercy, for this reason, that in me, as the foremost, Jesus Christ might display his perfect patience as an example to those who were to believe in him for eternal life." (RSV)*

INTRODUCTION

I and 2 Timothy and the book of Titus, are called the Pastoral Epistles. Timothy and Titus were both converted to Christianity under the teaching and preaching of Paul, the apostle to the Gentiles. *(Acts 16; Gal 2:3, RSV)* As disciples and co-workers of Paul they looked to Paul for leadership and direction, especially when they met resistance and false teachers within the communities they were sent to evangelize and oversee on Paul's behalf. *(I Tim 1:3-4; Tit 1:5, RSV)*

When Paul was in prison for preaching the gospel message, he could always depend on Timothy, Titus and Epaphroditus to get his word out and carry messages to the other Churches. While traveling on his missionary journeys, sometimes Timothy and Titus were responsible for carrying a letter from Paul to help settle a dispute in the Church. They sometimes functioned as mediators and peacemakers. When Paul was banned from a city, by the people in power he would send Timothy or Titus back to that city to smooth over the situation in his absence. *(Rom 16:21; 2 Cor 8:6, 16; Phil 2:25, RSV)*

Paul's first letter to Timothy is written while he is in prison in Philippi. Timothy is in Ephesus at this time and is being seriously challenged by false teachers who want to change the gospel they heard from Paul to their own advantage. Timothy is feeling overwhelmed and sends news to Paul about his situation, seeking advice and Paul's wisdom about how to handle the false teachers without causing irreparable damage to the congregation in Ephesus. *(I Tim 1:3, RSV)*

Paul knows all too well what Timothy is going through. For on numerous occasions he was challenged physically and verbally on his teaching that the way to salvation was through Jesus and Jesus alone. This theological position is known as *justification by faith alone.*

Paul gives Timothy the authority to act on what he was taught and not back down to the challenges he was facing. *(I Tim 1:18-19, RSV)* To back down now would threaten the stability of the new Christian movement. So rather than keep repeating his position, Paul writes a letter to Timothy that was to be read to the entire Church in Ephesus.

In this letter he used himself as an example of how faith in Jesus the Christ could turn one's life totally around. *(I Tim 1:12-14, RSV)* Your past does not matter. God's mercy eliminated the judgment we were due by allowing his Son, Jesus to die on the cross for all our sins, for our redemption. Paul's expression of gratitude can be summed up in this statement: *"Thank God for mercy!"* His gratitude is the beginning of our text this morning. With all we have let us give thanks, for, Paul reminds us to *thank God for mercy.*

As we see how mercy plays a major role in Paul's life, let us reflect and reminisce about the role mercy has played in our lives.

---

1)

Paul wasted no time instructing Timothy on what teachings are necessary to convince his audience and counterattack his opponents. The first lesson Timothy is to teach is that ***THROUGH MERCY WE ARE STRENGTHENED AND APPOINTED TO SERVICE.*** Read vv12-13,*"I thank him who has given me strength for this, Christ Jesus our Lord, because he judged me faithful by appointing me to his service, though I formerly blasphemed and a persecuted and insulted him; but I received mercy because I acted in ignorance and unbelief." (I Tim 1:12-13, RSV)*

In these verses Paul thanked Jesus for three things: **strength, trust, and a call to service.** Paul is all too aware of his history with the early Christians. He is very much aware of his former status as *persecutor of the Church.* Paul is not trying to hide or deny what he used to be. Instead, because he is so aware of his past, every time he thinks about all the Lord has done for him, it makes him burst out into thanksgiving and praise. *(I Tim 1:12, RSV)*

Paul calls himself a *blasphemer. (I Tim 1:13, RSV)* Now a blasphemer is the opposite of someone who blesses the name of God. It can be translated 3 ways: *to cut, to speak sharply against, and to utter a curse against.* Paul did all three!

Paul admits to being a violent man. Remember in the book of Acts, it was Paul who held the coats of those who stoned Stephen, the first Christian to die for Christ *(Acts 7:58, RSV)* Paul was on his way to Damascus to arrest Christians, have them imprisoned and tortured, put to death if they did not renounce their belief in Jesus as the Promised Messiah. *(Acts 9, RSV)*

Yet his present situation can be summarized in these few words: *"Look at me now! I have come a long way baby!"* God showed mercy on Paul because he was ignorant and did not believe Jesus was the Promised Messiah. It went against everything he had been taught to expect the Messiah to be like and to do. Paul trusted in the Law and his religious party (the Pharisees) more than the teachings of Jesus. Because he was wrong, he was ignorant and did not believe. *(I Tim 1:13, RSV)*

Paul gives himself as an example of the worse you could be and do against God and his Son. When he comes to the realization of his past mistakes, Paul wants to shout out, **THANK GOD FOR MERCY!**

As Christians we too must share our testimonies with others so they will be convinced that God's mercy is extended to everyone – whosoever will, let them come. *(Jn 3:16, RSV)* No prior religious experience required. No perfect past. No background checks. No empty closets *(we all have some skeletons in our closets we do not want others to see).* No height or weight requirements. No educational requirements. No recommendations needed. All sinners need to apply! It does not matter what color you are or what side of the tracks you came from. It does not matter if you had two parents, was raised by a single mom/dad, orphaned or put in foster care. Just come as you are!

We have all sinned and fallen short of God's glory. *(Rom 3:23, RSV)* If Jesus can save Paul, he can save you and I as well. So, let us not put on airs when others come to Christ, broken and lost. Let us just embrace them with love and say in unison, **THANK GOD FOR MERCY!**

_____

2)

Paul's reflection on his past mistakes brings to his mind another lesson Timothy should teach the believers in the city of Ephesus: ***THROUGH MERCY THE GRACE OF OUR LORD OVERFLOWED WITH LOVE.*** Read vv14-15, *"And the grace of our Lord overflowed for me with the faith and love that are in Christ Jesus. The saying is sure and worthy full acceptance, that Christ Jesus came into the world to save sinners. And I am the foremost of sinners." (I Tim 1:14-15, RSV)*

It was Paul who established the word ***grace*** *(charis)* in the Christian vocabulary. He used it over 100 times in his writings. *Grace* for Paul was an active force in his life that controlled both his thoughts and his actions. Paul knew that it was grace that knocked him to the ground that day on his way to Damascus to arrest Christians for had it been judgment, he would have died. *(Acts 9, RSV)*

Instead, God showed Paul mercy by calling him into his service as an apostle and giving him the strength that he would need to carry out his mission work. *Grace* for Paul always has two companions: *faith* and *love*. *Grace* presents us with the opportunity and option to be saved. Faith is our response to that *grace* and love shown to us by God and through us to others. This is the evidence that we have accepted God's mercy.

Paul assures Timothy that faith in Jesus is something you can put your trust and hope in. You can accept wholeheartedly the faith statement that Jesus came into the world to save lost sinners. Then to illustrate his point even further, Paul declares, *"I am the foremost of sinners; but I received mercy!"* Thank God for mercy! *(I Tim 1:15, RSV)*

God's mercy was apparent on Calvary's Hill. The Jews could not keep the laws of Moses. God sent Jesus as the ultimate sacrifice, the last lamb to be slain for the sins of the world. You know how you struggle daily with the flesh! You know some days you win, some days you lose! The law is always waiting to condemn us, convict us, and sentence us to eternal punishment. *(Rom 4:15, RSV)*

But those of us who have faith in Jesus, God's Son, every time we mess up mercy abounds, and judgment is rebuked and defeated again by the blood of Jesus. God knows that our hearts are not always filled with love, joy, thanksgiving or forgiveness. Thank God for mercy! Thank God that mercies are new every morning! *(Lam 3:23, RSV)*. Thank God for Jesus! Thank God for the Church of God! For although, like Paul, we may be the chief of sinners, God's mercy is still available to us. That is why John Newton, a sinner and slave trader penned these words after his conversion to Christianity, *"Amazing Grace, how sweet the sound, that saved a wrench like me. I once was lost, but now am found, was blind but now I see." (1725-1807 CE)* **THANK GOD FOR MERCY!**

---

3)

Paul's final piece of advice to help Timothy silence his enemies is to tell the believers ***THROUGH MERCY WE ARE SAVED TO BE WITNESSES OF HIS LOVE.*** Read vv16-17,*"But I received mercy for this reason that in me, as the foremost, Jesus Christ might display his perfect patience for an example to those who were to believe in him for eternal life." (I Tim 1:16-17, RSV)*

Paul saw his former life and his present life as an example for all who would become believers in the future. God used Paul to do his bidding and changed him from a respected persecutor for the Jews into a hated apostle to the Gentiles. If God could do that for Paul, he could do the same for anyone who accepts Jesus as the Christ. This is the gospel pure and simple. It was not complicated and bogged down with rules and rituals like Timothy's opponents tried to make it out to be.

Paul tells Timothy just keep it short and simple and to the point. There was no shame for Paul because what he did, he did out of ignorance and disbelief. Now the grace he received from God – even while in prison – was abundant. This same abundance was available to every hearer of the word.

Paul began this book with thanksgiving and ends with a doxology of praise. For to recognize that we have mercy on our side, is to be motivated to offer praises to our God. Paul declares God as King of all ages, eternal, invisible, the only God in the middle of false idol gods, due honor and glory from all his creation, now and forever, Amen! *(I Tim 6:14-16, RSV)*

That is what happens when we fully understand the magnitude of the role of mercy in a believer's life. This is the mercy of God that takes the initiative of grace – in other words, approaches us in our state of unbelief, sin, and disdain for righteousness – and offers to wipe the slate clean, forget all that we have done in the past and cast it into the sea. *(Micah 7:19, RSV)*

All you do in return is to believe in Jesus and that he came into the world to save sinners. THANK GOD FOR MERCY! Thank God for mercy! Mercy leads to faith and faith leads to prayer and prayer leads to forgiveness and forgiveness puts us back on the tract to love for another day.

Will you accept God's mercy today? It is available now, but it will not be extended forever. God bless you!

THE SECOND LETTER
TO TIMOTHY

(Disputed)

Sound Advice to Live By

SOUNDING OFF FOR JESUS!

2 TIMOTHY 4:2-5, *"Preach the word, be urgent in season and out of season, convince, rebuke, and exhort, be unfailing in patience and in teaching. For the time is coming when people will not put up with sound teaching, but having itching ears they will accumulate for themselves teachers to suit their own likings, and will turn away from listening to the truth and wander into myths. As for you, always be steady, endure suffering, do the work of an evangelist, fulfill your ministry." (RSV)*

INTRODUCTION

When you hear the phrase *SOUNDING OFF* it usually brings to mind an image of either putting somebody in their place, the housewives of Atlanta call it, *"throwing shade,"* or bringing something to an end like a radio or TV broadcast. The emphasis is on speaking and listening, in order to get one's point across. Therefore, the words are not necessarily *sound* in the sense of truth or life lessons, but rather an expression of opinions and criticisms. However, in our message this morning we will learn that *SOUNDING OFF FOR JESUS* is a positive expression for remaining true to the teachings of the Bible and the promptings of the Holy Spirit.

In this text, Paul is speaking to Timothy and supporting his decisions as a pastor because he is aware that Timothy received sound doctrine from both his mother Eunice, and his grandmother Lois. *(II Tim 1:5-6, RSV)* It is all in the teaching. As women, we have been given the responsibility of making sure our children and grandchildren know what the Lord expects of them, whether they stick to it or not. Proverbs 22:6 tells us, *"Train up a child in the way he should go, and when he is old, he will not depart from it." (RSV)*

Our text is about *sounding off for Jesus.* Paul gives sound advice to Timothy, building on what he was taught as a child. Timothy was a disciple of Paul and it was Paul who circumcised Timothy, because his father was Greek, but his mother was Jewish. Paul did not want to give any of the Jewish leaders, reason to criticize or ostracize Timothy from the synagogue or other Jewish gathering places. *(Acts 16:3, RSV)*

Paul and Timothy were co-workers for Christ. They traveled together on two missionary journeys, teaching and preaching the word of God, as Paul felt led by the Holy Spirit and the resurrected Christ. When Timothy accepted the call to preach under Paul, he became Paul's *son in the ministry. (Acts 16:1-5, RSV)* So for Paul it was of utter most importance that, as he approached the end of his own ministry, and perhaps his life, Timothy remained firm and steadfast in the sound teachings that he received from Paul.

Let us examine our text more closely so we too can sound off for Jesus.

---

1)

The first lesson we receive from our text is in order to hold on to sound doctrine **_WE MUST TEACH WITH CONVICTION._** Read v2, *"Preach the word, be urgent in season and out of season, convince, rebuke, and exhort, be unfailing in patience and in teaching." (II Tim 4:2, RSV)*

The early Christian Church was dynamic and powerful in its influence due to the coming of the Holy Spirit. *(Acts 2:41-42, RSV)* Others were jealous of its popularity and tried to imitate its message, sugar coating it for its audiences' pleasure, distorting it when they did not agree with the message of the resurrection. Some taught Gnosticism – the belief that everything in the world is evil, only things of the spirit were good.

Then Paul tells Timothy to preach and teach the gospel that he learned from his mother, grandmother, and Paul. *(II Tim 15, RSV)* This was sound doctrine that would never fail him. We must never alter the word of God to appease the audience. If the truth hurts, then take the pain and change the behavior! The truth shall set you free from the bondage of sin and bad habits. *(Jn 8:32, RSV)*

The Elders in our day did not allow us to do whatever we wanted to do in their presence. They would convince, rebuke, and exhort to return us to proper behavior that comes from belief in sound teachings. Yet today we allow everybody and anybody to do whatever they want to do in the Church. We allow them to dress however they want to dress, speak however they want to speak, and think it is cute, hip and acceptable. We allow it because *"we do not want to run the young folks away from the Church."* Teach sound doctrine and the Holy Spirit will be on your side! *(II Tim 4:3, RSV)* The Church does not conform to the world's standards, but the Church must transform and reform the world to God's standards. *(Rom 12:2, RSV)*

Going to Church use to be a measure of one's character. Today some say it is out of style; too many errands to do on Sunday; we need to rest from working all week; it is my family time; I cannot tithe because I need to pay my bills first. I have heard all the excuses in my 46 years of ministry.

However, what was true for Timothy and Paul back then, is still true for us today. Everybody does not want to hear the word of God! The word will convict you if you have given in to unsound doctrine. *(II Tim 4:14, RSV)* Therefore, as Christians we must teach with conviction the lessons we learned through the Church and through our parents. Non-believers may not want to hear it but sound off for Jesus anyhow!

2)

Our second lesson from the text is that ***EVERYTHING THAT SOUNDS GOOD TO YOU, IS NOT GOOD FOR YOU.*** Read v3,*"For the time is coming when people will not endure sound teaching, but having itching ears they will accumulate for themselves teachers to suit their own likings."(II Tim 4:3, RSV)*

From the days of the Old Testament prophets, people in positions of power have only wanted to hear pleasant comforting words of encouragement. When the false prophets spoke pleasant words from the Lord they would be condemned *(Jer 5:12; 27:16-17; 28:15-17, RSV)* However, when a prophet spoke out against the people's idolatry, sexual immorality, and corruption, they faced dire consequences, even death. This was true in Paul's day as well. *(Jer 11:21-23; 26:7-9; Acts 23:12, RSV)*

Therefore, it behooves the person who wants to basically stay well and alive, to only speak good words and bring encouraging words from the Lord to those in power. It did not matter what it sounded like, for as long as it was a positive word and you said it with a smile on your face.

Today you can just about hear anything and everything on television, the radio, CD, DVD, IPads, computers, and the newspaper. Our world is full of negative sound bites. Technology was supposed to be for our advancement. Instead, it has allowed every evil, malicious, sick, and perverted message in the hearts and minds of people to be broadcast.

Thoughts that people were once medicated for having, are now promoted and published on the Internet, or shown on TV, during prime time! It has been argued that this is freedom of speech. Yet they petition to get religious programming off the air!

But where will it end? Why do some things good to you end up being bad for you? Is there nothing sacred anymore? Our children can quote lyrics from "gangsta" hip-hop records, but do they know the words to the 23rd Psalm? Do they know the Lord's Prayer or the Apostle's Creed?

If we are going to make a difference in this world, as believers holding on to sound doctrine, we must promote and teach sound doctrine, not doctrine that divides ethnic groups, genders, or age groups. We cannot remain silent while our children are being misled about their heritage and potential for greatness.

When we hear the untruths, we must intercept them, counter them with the truth that comes from sound doctrine, and not accept it on face value. Just because somebody speaks it, who has a position of authority, does not make it sound doctrine or the truth for that matter. There is so much propaganda, aimed at dividing and destroying our belief in the word of God. Let us stand and see it for the evil that it is. *Because everything that sounds good to you, is not good for you!*

It is up to us to study God's word and pray that the truth and soundness of the word will penetrate our very being. *(II Tim 2:15, RSV)* Only then will we be able to stand against the wiles of the devil. *(Eph 6:11, RSV)* This is good advice for believers holding on to sound doctrine while sounding off for Jesus.

3)

Paul's third lesson of advice to his friend Timothy is to **_REMAIN SOBER, NO MATTER WHAT THE COST._** Read v5, *"As for you always be steady, endure suffering, do the work of an evangelist, fulfill your ministry." (II Tim 4:5, RSV)*

The tone of the letter is meant to move the hearers from a final message of warning to a challenge of sober mindedness. *(II Tim 4:1-2, RSV)* Paul commends Timothy and others addressed in the letter, to an unashamed commitment to the gospel and to the potential suffering that such commitment brings. *(II Tim 1:11-12, RSV)*

Paul should know. He was beaten 3 times *(2 Cor 11:25, RSV)*, thrown in jail multiple times *(Acts 16:25-26, RSV)*, ostracized by the Jews – his own people *(2 Cor 11:32, RSV)*, run out of town by some angry Gentile merchants, who practiced witchcraft, sorcery, and sold idol statues *(Acts 14:4-7, RSV)*, shipwrecked 3 times *(2 Cor 11:25, RSV)*. Now Paul was awaiting his own fate in Rome. Have his 9 lives run out? Whatever the outcome, Paul was ready to receive his fate for having preached the gospel and having served as an ambassador for Christ. *(Eph 6:20, RSV)*

Paul does not pull any punches when it comes to telling the truth about working for the Lord. Yet, he believes and tells Timothy that the rewards are greater than the suffering if you remain steadfast and sober. The concept of steadfastness means patient and anchored, no matter what the storm. Sober meant keeping your head, observe careful judgment, and self-control. Paul knew you needed to be both sober and anchored in order to finish this Christian journey, and not fall for unsound doctrine.

False prophets and teachers are always lurking around, seeking whom they can confuse, devour, upset, persuade, or mislead. It is good advice for believers to stay clear of false prophets, who try to look good by spewing an adulterated gospel of Jesus into the community.

Our communities need us to come together as one, as the Son and the Father are one. There is no time or energy for us to fight one another. For Paul said in Gal 3:28, *"In Christ there is no male or female, no Jew or Greek, no slave or free." (RSV)*

This is sound doctrine that we all must teach and emulate in society and especially in the Church. When we speak the truth of the Gospel, we are *SOUNDING OFF FOR JESUS!* What is *sound doctrine?* "That God so loved the world that he gave his only Son, that whoever believes in him shall not perish but have eternal life." *(Jn 3:16, RSV)*

What is *sound doctrine?* That "Jesus is the Way, the truth and the life, and no one comes to the Father but through him." *(Jn 14:6, RSV)* What is *sound doctrine?* That Jesus was crucified, buried, and on the third day arose from the dead. Now that is *sound doctrine!* Do not accept anything less than the best.

Yes, the enemy will try to silence you and shut you down, but just keep on *sounding off for Jesus!* God bless you!

THE LETTER TO TITUS

(Disputed)

Change Is Gonna Come!

ALLOWING THE HOLY SPIRIT
TO CHANGE YOUR LIFE

TITUS 3:4-7, *"But when the goodness and loving kindness of God our Savior, appeared, he saved us, not because of deeds done by us in righteousness, but in virtue of his own mercy, by the washing of regeneration and renewal in the Holy Spirit, which he poured out upon us richly through Jesus Christ our Savior, so that we might be justified by his grace and become heirs in hope of eternal life."(RSV)*

INTRODUCTION

The book of Titus is one of Paul's 3 Pastoral Letters. Timothy and Titus were both disciples of Paul and found salvation through his teaching and preaching of the Gospel message. This letter is addressed to Titus, who was a key mediator between Paul and the Corinthian Church during a time of turmoil and miscommunication (*2 Cor 2:13; 7:6-7, 13-15, RSV*).

Titus was the pastor of the Church on the island of Crete. Crete is an island off the coast of Italy. It is believed by many that Paul wrote this letter to Titus while in a Roman prison. Although Paul was physically bound, he always found the strength, faith, and hope to encourage his fellow workers in the vineyard.

It was Paul who left Titus in Crete to organize the Christian community there and promote Christian behavior over and against the behavior of the flesh. *(Tit 1:5, RSV)* The new converts were called to a life that was to be reflective of the Lord Jesus Christ. Remember we were first called Christians at Antioch, because the people noticed the followers of Jesus were acting Christ-like.*(Acts 11:26, RSV)* This new lifestyle was evidence of one's rebirth through baptism and only possible through the pouring out of the Holy Spirit. *(Jn 3:5-6, RSV)*

Here Titus is charged to "put things in order" and that requires a godly, commendable life outside as well as inside, the believing community. Unbelievers were watching and waiting to see if the converts were real, or in it only for the money and prestige like the traveling philosophers of his day.

Therefore, Paul instructs his disciple Titus to remind the believers in Crete that they must allow the Holy Spirit to change their lives so they can be in sync with our role model, Jesus the Christ. Then we too will be the kind of witnesses God requires us to be. Let us now look to Titus and examine how the Holy Spirit makes a difference in our lives.

----

1)

The first lesson we learn from our text is that when we allow the Spirit to change our lives, ***WE ARE READY FOR EVERY GOOD WORK.*** Read vv1-3, *"Remind them to be submissive to rulers and authorities, to be obedient, to be ready for any honest work, to speak evil of no one, to avoid quarreling, to be gentle, and to show perfect courtesy toward all men." (Tit 3:1-3, RSV)*

The book of Titus emphasized a concern for the unsaved and sees the good work of believers as a part of God's redemptive plan for the whole world. Here, Paul gives Titus instructions on how to put things in order according to the religious teachings he received from Paul. *(Tit 3:1-2, RSV)*

As Gentile believers, they can no longer partake in riotous living. They must now surrender all to Jesus and live the life of a Christian. A paramount charge to the new converts is that they perform *good works* towards others, especially to the household of faith. They are not to speak evil of anyone. They are told to avoid unnecessary arguing. Instead be gentle in your communications to others. Show courtesy and remember you are representing Christ always. The joy in our heart should attract others to Christ. Your kindness and your generosity towards others make you ready for every good work. *(Tit 3:2-5, RSV)*

Now Paul knows that the bar is set high, but he reminds Titus that we too were once sinners on display. We too were once foolish, disobedient, led astray, slaves to our passions and desires, living in malice and envy, hating one another for no reason, but the color of their skin, their sexual orientation, religious belief, or their accents. *(Tit 2:7-9, RSV)* It is in our nature to be disobedient! We inherited this behavior from our ancestors – Adam and Eve. *(Gen 3:11, RSV)*

It comes naturally. Paul says we were despicable! And Paul, of all people, should know! Therefore, as Christians and followers of the Way of Jesus the Christ, our lives can no longer look like it did before we were saved, before we came out of darkness and into God's marvelous light. *(I Pet 2:9, RSV)* That is why we confess and testify that a wonderful change has come over us since we met our Lord and Savior, Jesus the Christ.

But the change must start from the inside then spread to the outside. When that happens, we can say, *"for he who is in you is greater than he who is in the world." (I Jn 4:4 RSV)* Then somebody will see the difference Christ has made in your life and lifestyle. You do not have to go and shout it from the rooftops that you are saved. It will be obvious to all who you come in contact.

Then you will be able to embrace every good work with the help of the Holy Spirit. If your words do not match your behavior, if you have no good deeds to present before God on the Day of Judgment, then you are not filled with the Holy Spirit! *(Gal 6:8-10, RSV)* Actions speak louder than words! The Christian journey is not about you, for only what you do for Christ will count in the end.

2)

The second lesson we learn when we allow the Spirit to change our lives is that **_WE GET NONE OF THE CREDIT._** Read vv4-5,*"But when the goodness and loving kindness of God our Savior appeared, he saved us, not because of deeds done by us in righteousness, but in virtue of his own mercy, by the washing of regeneration and renewal in the Holy Spirit." (Tit 3:4-5, RSV)*

Paul continues to teach Titus the basics of the work of the Holy Spirit. He reminds Titus of the words he uttered to I Timothy (1:9), *"Who saved us and called us with a holy calling, not in virtue of our works, but in virtue of his own purpose and grace…" (RSV)*

Once we accepted Jesus as our Lord and Savior, we opened our hearts to the pouring out of the Holy Spirit into our lives. This pouring suggests volumes of God's Holy Spirit covering every aspect of our lives. You see the Holy Spirit does not compartmentalize its effect on our lives. It spills over in our work, home, friends, play, vacation, relationships, everywhere we move and have our being.

The Spirit cannot be contained, for the Bible says, *"Do not quench the Spirit" (I Th 5:19, RSV)* so whenever and wherever the Holy Spirit sees a need, it pours out a blessing, a healing. It teaches us to forgive one another; it teaches us to praise God anyhow! No matter the situation, we can say in the words of Job, *"All the days of my appointed time will I wait, till my change come." (Job 14:14, KJV)*

We need to pray because prayer connects us to the source of the pouring, which is God Almighty. We need to know how God want us to respond to the pouring, to the anointing. What good deed is waiting for our participation, our validation, our affirmation, and our confirmation?

We can never take credit for our own salvation. All we can own up to is having the good sense to come to God while we still have a chance. All we can brag about is receiving and accepting the call from Jesus, who said in his word, *"Come unto me, all you who labor and are heavy laden, and I will give you rest. Take my yoke upon you, and learn from me, for I am gentle and lowly in heart, and you will find rest for your souls. For my yoke is easy and my burden is light." (Mt 11:29, RSV)*

When we are brokenhearted, the Holy Spirit becomes available to us in ways we never acknowledged before. So many of us run from God's love, like Jonah *(Jon 1:3, RSV)*, instead of turning to God for healing and forgiveness like David *(Ps 51, RSV)* But God has not given up on us. No, no! His Spirit is everywhere we look, beckoning us to turn our lives over to our Creator. The season of Pentecost reminds us of what can happen if we allow the Holy Spirit to change our lives! *(Acts 2, RSV)*

You see, even after we have accepted Christ, we still do not know how to pray! The Holy Spirit intercedes on our behalf and interprets our words, so they are palatable to God's hearing. *(Rom 8:26-27, RSV)* Then God can respond to our every need as well as the desires of our heart. *(Ps 37:4, RSV)* Are you allowing the Holy Spirit to change your life, or are you trying to keep one foot in the world? Jesus said, *"No servant can serve two masters; for either he will hate the one and love the other, or he will be devoted to the one and despise the other. You cannot serve God and mammon." (Lk 16:13, RSV)*

---

3)

Our third and final lesson teaches us that when we allow the Holy Spirit to change our earthly lives, **_WE CAN NOW INHERIT ETERNAL LIFE._** Read vv6-7,*"…which he poured out upon us richly through Jesus Christ our Savior, so that we might be justified by his grace, and become heirs in hope of eternal life."(Tit 3:6-7, RSV)*

The Holy Spirit is rarely mentioned in the Pastoral Letters. But here Paul states that the Holy Spirit has been poured out on us richly through Jesus our Savior. Why? So that having been justified by his grace – not our good works or deeds – but by God's grace shown to us through his precious Son, we become heirs to eternal life. *(Tit 3:6, RSV)*

This grace connects us to God through spiritual adoption. The spiritual adoption takes place in Jn 3:16, *"For God so loved the world that he gave his only Son, that whoever believes in him should not perish, but have eternal life."(RSV)* Once we accept the terms of God's contract for grace, we become sons and daughters of God! We become brothers and sisters of Christ! Then, to take it even further, all power has been given over to us by the Master himself! We can say to any obstacle in our path – "MOVE!" - and that obstacle must get out of our way.

Paul tells us in Gal 3:29, *"And if you are Christ's, then you are Abraham's offspring, heirs according to the promise."* *(RSV)* Then in Gal 4:7, *"So through God you are no longer a slave, but a son, and if a son, then an heir."* *(RSV)* There is a saying that applies here, *"Blood is thicker than water."* This is extremely true because the blood of Jesus opened the gates of heaven on our behalf! Through the shedding of his blood on Calvary, we are now heirs to all the promises made to those who came before us and did not experience their fulfillment. *(Heb 11:39, RSV)*

But you are only eligible if you allow the Holy Spirit to enter your heart and change your life. Our ancestors said it this way, *"If you make one step, God will make two!"* Will you allow the Holy Spirit to take control of your life today? Are you ready to say yes to every good work, and give God all the glory? Then you can inherit eternal life because the Holy Spirit changed your earthly life. God bless you!

THE LETTER TO PHILEMON

(Undisputed)

No Slaves in the Kingdom!

THE TRUTH WILL SET YOU FREE!

PHILEMON 1:8-16, *"Perhaps this is why he was parted from you for a while, that you might have him back forever, no longer as a slave, but more than a slave, a beloved brother, especially to me but how much more to you, both in the flesh and in the Lord." (15-16, RSV)*

INTRODUCTION

Many scholars believe that the Apostle Paul is in jail again for doing the work of the Lord. But this did not hinder him from continuing his work of the Gospel through his disciples. Through the act of letter writing, Paul was able to teach, encourage, and advise those under his spiritual and physical care.

Paul is supported by several of his disciples who are not in jail. One such disciple is a recent convert – Onesimus. They have become close companions and Paul sees Onesimus as his *"son in the ministry."* Through this close relationship Paul has learned about Onesimus' troubled past, knowing that having one's past unresolved can affect how one conducts their current behavior and relationships.

Paul then decides he would intervene on Onesimus' behalf and try to reconcile two brothers in Christ – Onesimus a runaway slave, with Philemon, his master. Paul decides to take an approach of love rather than of duty. Paul's primary argument is the grace and forgiveness of God that covers all of us despite of our sins and shortcomings. This elevates us from the status of slave to that of brother and sister in Christ. *(Philem 1:16, RSV)*

Many religious interpreters have assumed over the years that Onesimus was a runaway slave and that the letter supports the institution of slavery. It was often read to slaves by the plantation preacher to promote submission to the master. Still today, there are those who are convinced that slavery is supported by this letter. But I am here to argue the opposite. Once we have accepted Jesus Christ as Lord and Savior over our lives, we are no longer slaves but fellow workers in Christ. Let us now listen for a word from the Lord that declares ***THE TRUTH SHALL SET YOU FREE!***

1)

The first lesson we learn from our text is that **_WE ARE NO LONGER SLAVES BECAUSE OF GOD'S LOVE._** Read vv8-9, *"Accordingly, though I am bold enough in Christ to command you to do what is required, yet for love's sake I prefer to appeal to you – I, Paul, an ambassador and now a prisoner also for Christ Jesus."(Philem 1:8-9, RSV)*

Paul reminds Philemon of their prior relationship as co-workers in Christ. He wants Philemon to remember their relationship and how he found the Lord because of Paul's teachings. In order to reintroduce himself to Philemon, Paul brings Philemon's own decision to follow Christ to his memory. In this way Paul is making his argument for the benefits of receiving Christ as Lord and Savior over one's life. This will help Paul ease into his position of support for Onesimus, Philemon's runaway slave.

Because of his status as Philemon's "Pastor" Paul could have pulled rank and ordered Philemon to receive Onesimus back as an equal, not as a servant. However, Paul chose instead to make an appeal for Onesimus based on *love*, not ownership. *(Philem 1:8, RSV)*

The Bible says, *"Love covers a multitude of Sins."(I Pet 4:8, RSV)* So if Philemon's perspective is that Onesimus has sinned against him, Paul takes on the argument of love rather than judgment, which leads to punishment. Forgiveness and acceptance are major components of love. *(I Cor 13:4—7, RSV)* Paul chose love as the olive branch to reconcile Philemon to Onesimus. *(Philem 1:7, RSV)*

The love of God is the only pathway to forgiveness, mercy, and our salvation. Paul knew the punishment for an escaped slave was death or severe torture. That is not what he wanted for Onesimus who now has become extremely useful to Paul while he was in jail. *(Philem 1:11, RSV)*

Since Onesimus' conversion, he is no longer a slave, but a brother in Christ! His status has changed because of the love of God shown to believers through his Son, Jesus the Christ. Believers are not slaves! God delivered us when he sent his Son to Calvary. Do not allow the world to bind you to sin and confusion. Just accept Jesus in your heart and be saved. As Jesus told Zacchaeus in the sycamore tree, *"...Today salvation has come to this house..."* (LK 19:9, RSV) Know that the truth will set you free. *(Jn 8:32, RSV)*

2)

The second lesson we learn from the text is that **_WE ARE NO LONGER A SLAVES BECAUSE WE NOW HAVE A PURPOSE._** Read vv11-13, (*"Formerly he was useless to you, but now he is indeed useful to you and to me.) I am sending him back to you, sending my very heart. I would have been glad to keep him with me, in order that he might serve me on your behalf during my imprisonment for the gospel." (Philem 1:11-13, RSV)*

Paul had benefitted from Onesimus' service and companionship. There is too little that we know about Onesimus' situation but the little that Paul reveals in this letter is positive. Yes, he ran away but his life has been changed, turned completely around since he gave his life to Christ.

Paul now refers to him as his *"child"* and he has become extremely useful in Paul's ministry. *(Philem 1:10, RSV)* In Paul's mind, Onesimus is more useful now as a servant of Christ, than he was as a slave for Philemon. As Philemon's slave, Onesimus performed tasks that benefited Philemon's earthly existence. Now as a witness for Christ, he is performing the greater task of bringing souls back to God.

It was Paul's desire to keep Onesimus with him, but he realized that Onesimus, though free through his faith in Jesus Christ, was an earthly slave and the property of someone else. Paul could have faced charges for harboring a runaway slave, and he had enough problems of his own.

Paul decides to contrast how useful Onesimus is now versus how useful he was as Philemon's slave. *(Philem 1:16, RSV)* Being a witness for Christ is serving a higher purpose in the universe. God freed Onesimus for a purpose. We were born for a mission. Others may recognize that gift and purpose sometimes before we do. But once you accept it, that truth will set you free. *(Jn 8:32, RSV)*

As believers, we were created with a purpose. Perhaps your purpose is the gift of teaching. Perhaps your purpose is the gift of medical diagnosis. Perhaps your purpose is the gift of proclamation. You do not have to be a preacher to tell somebody that Jesus saves.

Perhaps your purpose is to use your gift of knowledge about car repairs, plumbing, technology, or computers. Whatever it is, you were born for a purpose. You are not a mistake! You are not an accident. You were made in the image and likeness of God and God "don't make junk!"

Pray to the Holy Spirit to reveal your purpose to you so your living is in sync with God's will for your life. When you know your purpose – that truth will release you to be all that you can be for Christ.

---

3)

Our final lesson teaches us that ***WE ARE NO LONGER SLAVES, BUT MEMBERS OF GOD'S FAMILY.*** Read vv15-16,*"Perhaps this is why he was parted from you for a while, that you might have him back forever, no longer as a slave but more than a slave, a beloved brother, especially to me but how much more to you both in the flesh and in the Lord."(Philem 1:15-16, RSV)*

Paul does not make his appeal to Philemon based on the law. The Old Testament law addressed only Hebrew slaves. *(Exo 21:1-11, RSV)* The Roman law dealing with Gentile slaves was more hostile. Most slaves under Roman law were considered property and had no legal personhood. They would never be freed. *(Wikipedia, Slavery in ancient Rome)* Instead Paul chose to base his argument on the kind of love and forgiveness that runs through the bloodline of a family. Onesimus is no longer your slave, but a child of God, a member of the family. *(Philem 1:10, RSV)*

This kind of love that Paul is advocating is called *agape* love. It is the kind of unconditional love that a mother has for her disobedient and wayward child, who keeps testing her love over, and over again.

Paul loved Onesimus and Philemon for they both found salvation because of his preaching about the love God has shown to the world by sacrificing his Son on the cross. We are now one family. We are one in the Spirit and one in the Lord – *"one Lord, one faith, one baptism." (Eph 4:5, RSV))* Our differences are man-made. God is the Father of us all. If you are his child, then you are connected! That means you cannot hate someone because of the outside color of their skin or what continent that person was born on.

God shows no partiality. *(Acts 10:34, RSV)* God blesses whom God chooses and rejects whom he chooses to reject. It is not for us to judge who is worthy to live or die. The Son of Man will do the separating in the end. *(Mt 25:31-32, RSV)*

When we learn this lesson as people living together on this planet, then the truth will set us free from lies and myths about one another. I will not fear you and you will not fear me. Until we stop treating one group of people as inferior because of how God made them look on the outside, this world will continue to suffer the consequences of God's wrath. God does not lie. *(Num 23:19, RSV)* His truth stands firm. What truth? - That all people are created equal. That truth will set us all free. Amen!

HEBREWS AND THE SEVEN CATHOLIC EPISTLES TO THE GENERAL CHURCH

Hebrews, James, 1 and 2 Peter, 1, 2, 3 John, Jude

THE LETTER TO THE HEBREWS

MADE PERFECT THROUGH SUFFERING

HEBREWS 2:10-18, *"For it was fitting that he, for whom and by whom all things exist, in bringing many sons to glory, should make the pioneer of their salvation perfect through sufferings." (RSV)*

INTRODUCTION

The Book of Hebrews was written by a pastor as a sermon to encourage the early Christian community to continue in faith and hope in the face of severe hardship. This sermon develops the image of Christ as the great High Priest who fulfills and completes the Jewish system of sacrifice through his calling, ministry, suffering, death, resurrection, and return to the Father.

The Book of Hebrews focuses on Christ's suffering, death and exaltation. For it is through suffering that Jesus was made perfect. *(Heb 5:8-10, RSV)* The author of Hebrews wants his audiences to understand the gravity of Jesus' suffering for them. It was not just a one, time event locked into the past. The benefits of his suffering are for all to receive throughout eternity.

The blood of Jesus not only covered those early Christians who lived over 2000 years ago, but it covers you and I today in 2020, and all those yet to be born in the future. How can that be true? Our text explains it more clearly. Let us listen with a heart to learn and receive God's word for our life situation.

---

1)

As we look at our text, we see that the Book of Hebrews is focused on who Jesus was, what his suffering meant for his audience, and how his suffering connects us to God. This is what we call in the scholarly world – Christology. The Book of Hebrews, therefore, highlights three benefits of Jesus suffering on our behalf.

The first benefit we learn is that ***SUFFERING LEADS TO MEMBERSHIP IN GOD'S FAMILY.*** Read vv10-12, *"For it was fitting that he, for whom and by whom all things exist,* *in bringing many sons to glory, should make the pioneer of their salvation perfect through sufferings. For he who sanctifies and those who are sanctified have one origin. That is why he is not ashamed to call them brethren, saying, 'I will proclaim thy name to my brethren, in the midst of the congregation I will praise you.'" (Heb 2:10-12, RSV)*

When we hear the word *"perfect"* we think flawless, without spot or blemish, no visible faults. But that is not the meaning of perfect in Hebrews. What is meant here in our text is *completion.* Jesus completed his mission on earth and returned to the Father to serve as an advocate on our behalf.

Jesus' perfection was achieved because of his suffering. When Jesus left heaven to come to earth, he experienced much rejection from those closest to him. His own people treated Jesus like an outcast. His immediate family thought he was suffering from an identity crisis. Jesus said, *"A prophet is not without honor, except in his own country, and among his own kin, and in his own house." (Mk 6:4, RSV)*

Yet, he tasted every suffering known to humankind in order to open the way for us to become members of the family of God. *(Heb 2:18, RSV)* In life he was able to conquer every temptation. *(I Cor 10:13, RSV)* This experience made him like us in every way. Because he led the way by his faithfulness to God, he offers sanctification to all who believe in him.

Those who believe are brought into the family of God through faith in his Son Jesus the Christ. Through Christ's suffering we are initiated into the family of God. When we suffer and trust that God will work it out, we prove that we are children of God.

The author of the Book of Hebrews preaches this message to his audience because some have turned their backs on the faith. They could no longer withstand the persecution, the being lied on, the being talked about. For those who left the suffering was too great a cost. Yet without suffering we remain in foster care. We cannot be adopted, grafted, born into the family of God unless we too suffer and pass the test. For it is only through suffering that we are made perfect. *(Heb 2:10, RSV)*

---

2)

A second benefit we learn we received as a result of Jesus' suffering is ***JESUS SHATTERED THE POWER OF THE DEVIL.*** Read vv14-15,*"Since, therefore, the children share in flesh and blood, he himself likewise partook of the same nature, that through death he might destroy him who has the power of death, that is, the devil, and deliver all those who through fear of death were subject to lifelong bondage."(Heb 2:14-15, RSV)*

In the Old Testament, one was obligated to obey the law, every commandment, every ordinance, and every statute. Not to do so meant punishment and curses. *(Lev 26:14-18, RSV)* Of course, the Law was broken by the masses, even some great men of God, such as Abraham, who lied and tried to pass off Sarah as his sister instead of his wife *(Gen 12:13, RSV)*; Noah who got drunk *(Gen 9:21, RSV)*; Moses who killed a man *(Exo 2:11-12, RSV)*; and David who committed adultery and murder *(2 Sam 11:4, 14, RSV)*. The inability to keep the Law produced great fear in the peoples' hearts. Remember Job? He prayed for his children daily just in case they sinned by omission or co-mission. *(Job 1:4-5, RSV)*

Bringing sacrifices to the Temple was an attempt on the part of the people and the priests to correct any violation against their soul and repair any gap between the worshiper and God. However, as centuries passed by, it became too little, too late, and God allowed Jerusalem to be destroyed and the people were carted off into Babylonian Exile. *(2 Kings 25, RSV)*

All this changed when Jesus left heaven and came to earth – what we call the incarnation – God taking on flesh. *(Jn 1:14, RSV)* Through his life's work believers can now be made perfect. *(Jn 1:12-13, RSV)* The age of offering sacrifices is over and all that is required now is to believe on Jesus the Christ and be saved. *(Rom 10:9, RSV)*

They were accustomed to doing things the old way- through animal and grain sacrifice - that they had a hard time fathoming a new way leading to salvation, and perfection. *(Lev 1-6, RSV)* This is why Jesus declared to his disciples when they confessed that they did not know the new way, *"I am the Way, the Truth and the Life; no one comes to the Father, but by me." (Jn 14:6, RSV)*

This new reality empowered people and they no longer were afraid to die a physical death. When Jesus conquered their fear of death, he conquered Satan's hold over them as well. *(I Cor 15:54-56, RSV)* Satan puts the fear of God in us, by telling us that we cannot keep the Law. Therefore, we are bound to sin and eternal punishment. But we know Satan is a liar! *(Jn 8:44, RSV)* Jesus conquered death and the devil on the cross. When they thought Jesus was lying in a borrowed tomb, Jesus descended into the lower parts of the earth. *(Eph 4:9, RSV)*

If Satan has power over you today it is because you have given it to him, for we are made perfect through Christ's suffering. There is still power in the blood, power in the blood of the Lamb of God, who takes away the sins of the world. *(Jn 1:29, RSV)*

---

3)

The final benefit of Christ's suffering that we learn from this text is that ***CHRIST BECAME OUR HIGH PRIEST.*** Read vv17-18, *"Therefore, he had to be made like his brethren in every respect, so that he might become a merciful and faithful high priest in the service of God, to make expiation for the sins of the people. For because he himself has suffered and been tempted, he is able to help those who are tempted"* (Heb 2:17-18, RSV)

It was the role of the High Priest to serve as the mediator between the people and God, and God and the people. In the Old Testament this was the role of the prophet. The High Priest in Jesus' day was human just like those whose sacrifices he received and offered to God. The High Priest was very aware of life's temptations and could relate when the people fell into sin and sought forgiveness.

Jesus wanted that same experience in order to be made perfect. He had divine experiences for he was with the Father from the beginning. *(Jn 1:1-2, RSV)* Yet, he could not know human temptations, human sufferings, human disappointments, the loss of loved ones, loneliness, weeping, sleep deprivation, abuse, torture, yes, even death, until he became a God-Man.

Because Jesus was fully human and fully divine serving as our High Priest means Jesus understands what we go through every day. He understands hunger, thirst, pain and sorrow, joy, and laughter. He experienced it all! This then qualifies Jesus in a unique way to serve as our High Priest.

When we go to him in prayer, he does not look at us as a judgmental condemning judge, but he remembers what it was like to be human and those memories invoke feelings of compassion and empathy. Jesus knows all about our struggles and he will guide us safely home to be with him when our time here on earth is over.

Jesus, as our High Priest, can relate to our every need. The old Indian Proverb says, *"Don't judge your brother or sister until you have walked a mile in their shoes."* Well, Jesus has walked more than a mile in our shoes. He walked all the way up Golgatha's Hill! He let them nail him to a cross. He let them place him in a borrowed tomb. But on the third day he let them know that all authority has been given to him. *(Mt 28:18, RSV)*

Our salvation is made perfect, complete, because of Christ's suffering. This means that we too must suffer if we want to reach perfection. If we chose to bypass the cross, there will be no crown to exchange. Remember, we are made perfect through suffering. God bless you!

THE LETTER FROM JAMES

Patience Is a Virtue!

PATIENCE IN SUFFERING

JAMES 5:7-11, *"Be patient, therefore, brethren, until the coming of the Lord. Behold the farmer waits for the precious fruit of the earth, being patient over it until it receives the early and the late rain. You also be patient. Establish your hearts, for the coming of the Lord is at hand." (RSV)*

INTRODUCTION

The Letter from James is one of the most controversial books of the New Testament. It is argued that it was written during pre-Christian and Jewish relations. It is not addressed to only one Church, but to numerous Churches in the diaspora. His style is instructional, and he uses ethical teaching to promote Christian behavior among those who are no longer in his geographical regions.

Some scholars argue that James' statement *"faith without works is dead" (James 2:17, RSV)* directly contradicts Paul's theology of justification by faith and faith alone. *(Rom 5:1, RSV)* But when one takes a closer look at this peculiar letter, one is called to check out one's own conduct and priorities. For James, the source of moral virtue is wisdom received from God. *(James 3:17, RSV)*

James writes this letter to the twelve tribes in the Dispersion. *(James 1:1, RSV)* After Jesus' ascension, to be a Christian was against the Roman law, a crime punishable by death. Christianity commanded loyalty only to the one supreme God, not to the Roman Emperors, who thought they were gods in human form. *(Exo 20:3, RSV)*

So those who believed in Jesus and practiced their faith were driven out of their homes for fear of being captured, persecuted, and tortured. They left Israel and Jerusalem and scattered all over the surrounding geographical areas, trying to find refuge and security. These are the people to whom James addressed his letter. James, believed to be the brother of Jesus, realized that the ones living in Dispersion needed instruction on how to live their lives apart from the community that gave them life, hope and encouragement. James counsels them to hold fast to their faith. *(James 1:2-4, RSV)* The temptation to give up before the goal is reached comes inevitably to all Christians at one time or another, especially those facing persecutions. James is telling his audience, and us today, do not give up! Do not quit! No matter how dark the road may seem, no matter how long the night, together with God's grace, we can make it.

Let us now revisit the words of James and apply them to our daily struggles as believers in a multi-cultural and pluralistic society.

_____

1)

The first lesson we learn from James' letter to those in the Dispersion is that **_WE MUST REMAIN PATIENT UNTIL CHRIST'S RETURN._** Read v7,"*Be patient, therefore, brethren, until the coming of the Lord. Behold the farmer waits for the precious fruit of the earth, being patient over it until it receives the early and late rain.*" *(Jas 5:7, RSV)*

James chose the image of a farmer as his illustration of patience and how patience eventually yields a harvest. He explains that when the farmer plants his seeds, he does not worry all season if the seeds are going to grow or how plentiful his harvest will be. All the farmer knows is that he did his part, his best, and now it was up to God to provide the harvest. Only God can provide the sunshine, only God can provide the rains. So why was he going to worry over something he had no control over? The farmer's attitude is to remain patient and trust God through the course of nature.

The same situation relates to us. If we do our best, give our all, witness to God's goodness throughout the community, then we need not worry about those who choose to put stumbling blocks in our path. In the face of tribulations our hearts are strengthened in knowing that the Lord is coming back soon. Until then, we strengthen our hearts through God's holy word, prayer, fasting, and fellowship with other believers. Therefore, James instructs us to be patient, for patience leads to endurance.

_____ .

2)

The second lesson James teaches the people of the Dispersion is that **_WE SHOULD NOT GRUMBLE AGAINST ONE ANOTHER._** Read vv 9-10,"*Do not grumble, brethren, against one another, that you may not be judged; behold, the Judge is standing at the doors. As an example of suffering and patience, brethren, take the prophets who spoke in the name of the Lord.*" *(Jas 5:9-10, RSV)*

James tells us not only to be patient as farmers, who have faith that the harvest will come, but also be steadfast as the prophets of old. You now everybody is always talking about how patient Job was, when if one reads the final chapters more closely, it would be obvious that even Job's patience was wearing thin. *(Job 23, RSV)* He argued with God about his justice and his absence during his entire ordeal. *(Job 40:1, RSV)* Yet, no matter what God permitted Satan to do to him, Job never gave up. Instead, he declared, *"Though he slay me; yet will I trust in him..." (Job 13:15, KJV)*

James reminds us that Jesus is watching us closely to see if we try to judge each another when he has not judged us. *(Jas 5:8-9, RSV)* Although sometimes in this life, we, too, fall on our knees and say the same words of Job in order to find strength to finish the journey. We live in an imperfect world where we are persecuted for many things – our skin color, our sexual orientation, our religious choices, but we know in our hearts that God will take care of us, so we need not grumble or complain. It will only put us in the seat of judgment. *(Jas 4:12, RSV)* God may not remove us from the situation, but God will give us the strength to get through it.

Therefore we should not grumble against one another, *"Have no anxiety about anything, but in everything by prayer and supplication with thanksgiving let our requests be made known to God."(Phil 4:6, RSV)* We see evidence of this with the Old Testament prophets, who faced all kinds of life threatening situations, but through it all they learned to trust God's will. Even while hanging on the cross, Jesus uttered these words, *"Father forgive them; for they know not what they do." (Lk 23:34, RSV)* If Jesus can say these words while nailed to a cross, we can certainly resist grumbling against whatever our neighbors do and say against us.

---

3)

The final lesson James teaches the people of the Dispersion is that ***IF WE REMAIN STEADFAST, WE WLL BE BLESSED!*** Read v11, *"Behold, we call those happy who were steadfast. You have heard of the steadfastness of Job, and you have seen the purpose of the Lord, how the Lord is compassionate and merciful." (Jas 5:11, RSV)*

James now uses Job as the picture of endurance and patience. Job's situation may have been dire initially – lost his children, his wealth, his friends, even his health - yet when his test was finally over and he remained steadfast, Job was rewarded 2-fold and lived to see four generations for all that he went through. His family was restored, his wealth was multiplied, and his standing in the community was never higher among family and friends. *(Job 42:10-12, RSV)*

The moral of the story is that if you remain steadfast and stand your ground, if you do not grumble against others, God will bless you in the end for your faithfulness. Your blessings will be obvious to those who try to persecute you and accuse you falsely *(like Job's 3 friends - Job 2:11, RSV)*. In the end you will be vindicated. God bless you!

THE FIRST LETTER FROM PETER

A Call To Holiness

LIVING THE RESURRECTED LIFE

I PETER 1:13-25, *"Therefore gird up your minds, be sober, set your hope fully upon the grace that is coming to you at the revelation of Jesus Christ. As obedient children, do not be conformed to the passions of your former ignorance, but as he who called you is holy, be holy yourselves in all your conduct; since it is written, 'You shall be holy, for I am holy'..." (RSV)*

INTRODUCTION

Peter writes this letter with the purpose of sketching a vision of the Christian life rooted in God's saving action through the death, resurrection, and glorification of Jesus the Christ. Peter assures his audience of their salvation and reminds them of the hope this generates for the community. The community is to live a life of integrity and love, risking suffering and alienation if necessary, for the sake and cause of Christ. *(I Pet 1:5-7, RSV)*

As we examine this scripture more closely, we will find lessons that will strengthen our faith and encourage us on this Christian journey.

1)

The first lesson we learn from our text is that ***THE RESURRECTED LIFE DELIVERS US FROM OUR DESIRES.*** Read vv13-16, *"Therefore gird up your minds, be sober, set all your hope fully upon the grace that is coming to you at the revelation of Jesus Christ. As obedient children, do not be conformed to the passions of your former ignorance, but as he who called you is holy, be holy yourselves in all your conduct; for it is written, 'You shall be holy, for I am holy.'" (I Pet 1:13-16, RSV)*

In vv 13-25, Peter shifts his focus from events concerning the end of time to ethical and moral responsibilities that believers now have as followers of Christ and recipients of the gospel message. He encourages them to *prepare their minds for action. (I Pet 1:13, RSV)*

In the time of the apostles, pulling up one's long robe and tying it around oneself, meant you were getting ready for action. In the Old Testament book of Exodus, those preparing to leave Egyptian slavery were told, *"In this manner you shall eat it: your loins girded, your sandals on your feet, and your staff in your hand; and you shall eat it in haste." (Ex 12:11, RSV)* This is the same urgency that Peter wants his audience to embrace in their relationship with Jesus and with one another. Jesus is their example. They no longer had to live in ignorance, like disobedient children. Christ taught a life-style superior to that followed by non-believers. *(I Pet 14, RSV)*

Our fleshy desires must be controlled by our hope and faith in the Redeemer. What we use to do before we got saved is in the past because we did not know any better. But now that we have heard the gospel truth, now that we have witnessed the holy life lived through our Savior; we no longer have any excuse for not trading in our life of sin and flesh for a holy life.

Lev 19:2 reads, *"You shall be holy, for I the Lord your God am holy." (RSV)* Holiness is the adjective that characterizes the day-to-day conduct of the believer always and everywhere, not just in Church on Sundays. Holy does not mean we will never make mistakes and fall. Rather being holy means every day, every week, every month, every year, we are striving to be more like Christ. We are giving up those things behind us and pressing on toward the mark of the prize of the higher calling, which is in Christ Jesus our Lord. *(Phil 3:14, RSV))* In the Methodist Church we call that *growing in grace*.

If we fall, we get back up! If you sin, ask for forgiveness and then repent. God will forgive you and cast your sins as far as the east is from the west. *(Ps 103:12, RSV)* Be holy as God is holy! *(Lev 11:44, RSV)* Living the resurrected life delivers us from our desires and makes it possible to walk in the path of righteousness as David declared in Psalm 23 *(Ps 23:4, RSV)*. A holy God demands a holy people.

The prophet Isaiah was terrified when he was brought into the heavenly Temple of the Most-High God. Isaiah declared, *"Woe is me! For I am lost; for I am a man of unclean lips and I dwell in the midst of a people of unclean lips; for my eyes have seen the King, the Lord of hosts!" (Isa 6:5, RSV)* Before God could use the prophet Isaiah, the seraph had to fly towards him and touch his mouth with a hot coal from the altar of God. This made Isaiah holy so he could proclaim God's word to the people. *(Isa 6:6-7, RSV)*

We cannot fix our hearts on worldly things or copy the people of this world, for we are just traveling through this barren land, trying to reach our eternal home. Are you living the resurrected life?

---

2)

The second lesson from our scripture is that **_THE RESURRECTED LIFE WAS BOUGHT AND PAID FOR BY THE FATHER._** Read vv17-19, *"And if you invoke as Father him who judges each one impartially, according to his deeds, conduct yourselves with fear throughout the time of your exile. You know that you were ransomed from the futile ways inherited from our fathers, not with perishable things such as silver or gold, but with the precious blood of Christ, like that of a lamb without blemish or spot."(I Pet 1:17-19, RSV)*

The new believers now have the privilege of calling God, "Father" because of their hope and faith in Jesus the Christ. *(I Pet 1:17, RSV)* Since he is their Father, too, they are to respond to his authority as obedient children. Now they are living in exile, which means they must await the return of Christ to bring them back home with him. However, the only reason they are eligible to enter the Kingdom of Heaven is because the Father paid for their sins through the sacrifice of his beloved Son. *(I Pet 1:3, RSV)*

Jesus' death on the cross was the last and final sacrifice, a perfect and sufficient sacrifice, for the sins of the whole world. *(Heb 7:27; 9:14, RSV)* You see the Roman custom was that a slave could pay money into a temple treasury so that the idol god, honored at the Temple, would purchase or ransom him. *(http://en.wikipedia.org/Slavery_in_ancient_Rome)* The newly freed slave would then be the property of that idol god, but in relation to society, a free person. Jesus paid our ransom for we were in bondage to sin and death.

This sin came through the DNA of Adam. *(Rom 5:12-14, RSV)* From their expulsion from the Garden of Eden until Jesus' death on the cross, perishable things were offered as a ransom for our sins. However, sheep, goats, pigeons, barley, and wheat offerings, were only temporary sacrifices. They had to be repeated every time the people fell short of the glory of God.

Therefore, God offered a once and for all sacrifice, to pay a final ransom for now and throughout all eternity. *(Heb 9:14, RSV)* You see slaves were redeemed through the exchange of gold and silver, earthly resources. *(I Pet 1:18-19, RSV)* But as slaves to sin, we needed something more spiritual and eternal. The precious blood of Jesus was the only ransom that could qualify and cover the costs.

Therefore, as sons and daughters of God, we owe him reverence, awe, fear, glory and praise. God has called us into a special relationship with him. He has called us out of the darkness of sin into the marvelous light of salvation and eternal life! *(I Pet 2:9, RSV)* If we accept this calling, we also accept God's mandate to live the resurrected life of obedience, hope, faith, and holiness. Are you living the resurrected life?

---

3)

Our third lesson is that ***THE RESURRECTED LIFE IS DRIVEN BY LOVE.*** Read vv22-23, *"Having purified your souls by your obedience to the truth for a sincere love of the brethren, love one another earnestly from the heart. You have been born anew, not of perishable seed but of imperishable, through the living and abiding word of God..." (I Pet 1:22-23, RSV)*

Peter addressed the people's ethical obligations to God earlier in the chapter. *(I Pet 1:21, RSV)* Now he addresses the ethical obligations we have to one another. Peter teaches the Gentile converts that because they have purified their souls through faith, obedience, and reverence to God, now they can truly show genuine love towards one another. *(I Pet 1:22, RSV)*

The recipients of this letter found themselves to be a threatened minority in a disbelieving and sometimes hostile community. *(I Pet 1:6, RSV)* Loving their enemies was a difficult task. However, Peter teaches that if the believer loves Christ, they must love one another just as much. When this is made a reality, then we can fulfill God's original purpose for his people, as it is stated in the summary of the Law, *"…You shall love the Lord your God with all your heart, and all your soul, and with all your strength, and with all your mind; and your neighbor as yourself."* (Lk 10:27, RSV)

We are called to love each other from the heart no matter what! Our affection towards one another must be constant and enduring, unshaken by adversity or changing circumstances. We love as Christians because the imperishable seed of Christ has been implanted within our hearts. This new seed transforms us into a new creation. We are born anew! *(I Pet 1:23, RSV)*

Just like blood runs through our human veins, the word of God pumps the gospel message through our spiritual veins and into our hearts, making us love our enemies as well as our friends. This word seed is enduring and everlasting. It is not like the seeds we use to plant flowers and grass. Here Peter quotes from Isaiah 40:8, *"The grass withers, the flower fades; but the word of our Lord will stand forever."* (RSV)

Let us crave for the word of God as a baby craves for its mother's milk. *(I Pet 2:2, RSV)* The more milk the baby drinks, the stronger and more mature the baby becomes. If we stay in the word, we too as the body of Christ, will grow spiritually and mature in our relationship with God and with others. Then we can live the resurrected life that Jesus calls us to live: *a life of obedience, hope, faith, and love!* God bless you!

PETER'S SECOND LETTER TO THE GENERAL CHURCH

Having the Final Word

THE LAST SAY

---

2 PETER 1:16-21, *"For we did not follow cleverly devised myths when we made known to you the power and coming of our Lord Jesus Christ, but we had been eyewitnesses of his majesty. For when he received honor and glory from God the Father and the voice was born to him by the Majestic Glory, saying, 'This is my beloved Son, with whom I am well pleased' we heard this voice born from heaven, for we were with him on the holy mountain." (RSV)*

INTRODUCTION

Years ago, if someone said they belonged to the Methodist Church their roots went back a few generations. They would have been well schooled in Methodist doctrine and belief. They would have come up through the ranks – beginning with the Buds of Promise *(a children's missionary group)*, then Sunday School.

Today unfortunately, that has all changed. People marry into the faith of their spouse or join because it is in a convenient location to where they live. Therefore, so that no one is unknowledgeable about what we believe as Methodists, the belief that I will address in this lesson is the belief in the Bible as the ultimate authority of our faith. *(The Book of Discipline of the A.M.E. Zion Church. A.M.E. Zion Church Publishing House, Charlotte, N. C. Articles of Religion, #V, p 14, 2008)* It is within the pages of the books of the Bible, that we learn about God's plan of salvation for a dying world.

The founder of Methodism was a religious Anglican priest named John Wesley. The son of a preacher and a strict religious mother, he also had a brother named Charles. Together they felt that the Anglican Church was lacking in the area of the Holy Spirit. John Wesley never intended to start a new Church movement; he only wanted to inject the power and dramatic presence of the Holy Spirit into the Anglican Church. But he was met with resistance and sometimes violence over the changes he wanted to implement. *(http://en.wikipedia.John_Wesley)*

As a committed Anglican priest Wesley insisted that the scriptures were our ultimate authority on God's will, God's direction, and God's purpose for our lives. For John Wesley and for many Methodist still today, the Holy Bible has the last say over our lives. It should be consulted before we make any decision that will affect our being and the lives of those we come in contact as well.

Our text highlights three reasons why the Methodist Church as well as other denominations, view the Bible as the unadulterated word of God, thereby having the last say. Let us look closely for Peter's explanation and support of this premise for his audiences.

---

1)

The first lesson we learn from our text is that ***AUTHORITY COMES FROM FIRST-HAND EXPERIENCE.*** Read v16, *"For we did not follow cleverly devised myths when we made known to you the power and coming of our Lord Jesus Christ, but we had been eyewitnesses of his majesty." (II Pet 1:16, RSV)*

Second Peter was written during a time when false prophets were springing up everywhere. He condemns those who create their own gospel from their own opinions. They had neither seen Jesus nor did they believe in his message. All they wanted was the prestige and the glory. Yet for Peter their teachings were unsubstantiated and misleading because they were not eyewitnesses to the truth. *(II Pet 1:16-18; 2:1-3, RSV)* The Apostles were with Jesus for three long years. They heard the voice from heaven saying, "This is my beloved Son, with whom I am well pleased." *(II Pet 1:17-18, RSV)* They saw him heal the sick and raise the dead. *(Jn 5:8-9; 11:43-44, RSV)* They witnessed him feeding 5000 with two fish and five loaves of bread. *(Jn 6:11-12, RSV)*

Even though all the disciples were not at the foot of the cross as were the women and John, they were close by and saw him nailed to the cross. *(Jn 19:25-26, RSV)* Then they saw him after the resurrection in the Upper Room and were able to put their fingers in the nail prints in his hands and their hand in his side. *(Jn 20:26-28, RSV)* These Apostles, these eyewitnesses knew the man the Bible tells us about for they themselves picked up their pens and wrote down what their eyes had seen, and their ears heard.

This gave the Apostles authority to speak about Jesus from firsthand experience. Their writings and the collection of their actions in the New Testament, all carry the authority of proclaiming the good news to us centuries later. The books of the Bible are the last words on the topic of God. That makes the Bible a Methodist's ultimate authority and therefore, God's word has the last say.

---

2)

The second lesson we learn about the Bible having the last say is that ***IT POSSESSES TIMELESS PROPHECY THAT FUNCTIONS IN OUR LIVES.*** Read v19 *"And we have the prophetic word made more sure. You will do well to pay attention to this as to a lamp shining in a dark place, until the day dawns and the morning star rises in your hearts." (II Pet 1:19, RSV)*

Many modern-day Churches and religions believe that the Old Testament is obsolete and irrelevant to the New Testament Christian. But that is not what Methodists believe. We believe the New Testament has ultimate authority because the Apostles were eyewitness. So too do we believe that the Old Testament has authority because it possesses timeless prophecy that functions in our lives as literal lamps in a world of darkness.

The Old Testament is the history, the research, and background, for our understanding of the New Testament. Jesus is the New Testament and Jesus came not to destroy but to fulfill the Old Testament. *(Mt 5:17, RSV)* When we try to learn and understand Jesus, his mission, his life and why the Jews rejected him, we must turn to the Old Testament as our authority and witness!

You cannot divorce one from the other! Jesus read the Old Testament prophecy about the mission of the Promised Messiah in the Temple *(Isaiah 58:6; 61:1-2, RSV)*, in order to announce his purpose here on earth. *(Luke 4, RSV)* Reading this Old Testament prophecy helped put his mission in perspective for those who were following the signs and the expected behavior of the Promised Messiah.

Jesus taught scripture with such power and authority that the people marveled. *(Mt 7:28-29, RSV)* For unlike the Pharisees and Sadducees, Jesus read the written word with power because he was the word taken on flesh. *(Jn 1:14, RSV)* Since the Old Testament began the story of salvation and Jesus finished the story, we believe as Methodists, that the Bible has *the last say.*

———————————

3)

Our final lesson from this text is that ***THE SCRIPTURES HAVE BEEN INSPIRED BY THE HOLY SPIRIT.*** Read vv20-21,*"First of all you must understand this, that no prophecy of scripture is a matter of one's own interpretation, because no prophecy ever came by the impulse of man, but men moved by the Holy Spirit spoke from God."(II Pet 1:20-21, RSV)*

The writers, editors, and compilers of the Bible did not just one day decide, "Hey let's write a religious book!" Peter tells us that no prophecy of scripture is an opinion, or interpretation. *(II Pet 1:20, RSV)* Therefore, as Methodists we believe that the Holy Scriptures are our ultimate authority because they have been inspired by the Holy Spirit! The Church Fathers and Mothers were all vessels of God's will. God gave them a message and they brought it to us.

The Bible, as our ultimate authority, contains all we need to attain salvation. *(Rom 10:8-9, RSV)* We do not need to subscribe to religious reality shows that might confound us or cause us to doubt the word of God. All we need for salvation is found in this Holy Book. It and it alone has the last say. For its message is eternal and its voice is that of the Holy Spirit.

A famous theologian by the name of Dwight L. Moody, once said about the Bible, *"Either this book will keep you from your sins, or your sins will keep you from this book."* The choice is up to us. But if you are a Methodist, the Bible still has the last say. We believe in a God who can scoop up some clay, blow his breathe into it and make a human being. We believe that a disobedient prophet got swallowed by a big fish and was regurgitated on the very beach he was running away from.

We believe a baby was born in Bethlehem, wrapped in swaddling clothes, placed in a manger, because there was no room for him and his parents in the Inn. *(Lk 2:1-7, RSV)* We believe that a crucified Savior, on the third day shook off his grave clothes and became a risen Lord! *(Jn 2:19, RSV)* But with God, all things are possible! *(Mt 19:26, RSV)*

We believe in these seemingly impossible events because God said it and men and women were inspired to record it for future generations to read, find salvation, power and eternal life in these very words. *(Jn 20:30-31, RSV)* And without faith it is impossible to please God. *(Heb 11:6, RSV)* Therefore, as Methodists, we believe the Bible has the last say! God bless you!

THE FIRST LETTER OF JOHN

ADOPTED INTO THE FAMILY OF GOD

REALIZING YOUR ESSENCE

I JOHN 3:1-3, *"See what love the Father has given us, that we should be called children of God; and so we are. The reason why the world does not know us is that it did not know him. Beloved we are God's children now; it does not yet appear what we shall be, but we know that when he appears, we shall be like him, for we shall see him as he is. (RSV)*

INTRODUCTION

The author of the first letter of John writes this letter with affection and concern for the spiritual welfare of those to whom it is addressed. The purpose of the letter is to deepen the spiritual life of its readers and to correct the heretical teachings of those who denied that God was in the person of Jesus the Christ. *(I Jn 1:1-4; 2:19, RSV)*

John was excited about what he had been taught about the true essence of Jesus as the Christ, the Promised Messiah and the Son of God. He wanted to share his good news with his family and friends. He wanted them to know that we now have fellowship with God the Father, God the Son, and God the Holy Spirit. *(I Jn 4:2, RSV)*

John believed that because we have fellowship with God, God brings us into fellowship with each other. *(I Jn 1:7, RSV)* This is the essence of our salvation. However, many Christians have been out of touch with their true essence and have lost contact with the source of their potential as human beings. Yet, we participate in a universe that has been programmed to always respond to the reality of its essence. The sun always acts like the sun and rises and sets on schedule. Yet, as human beings, we sometimes choose to be out of step with creation and thus fail to realize our true essence as creatures loved by the Creator.

When this happens the substance from which we were created – the earth – takes over and we become focused on satisfying the flesh instead of nurturing the spirit within us. *(Gen 2:7, RSV)* We ignore what the philosopher Aristotle calls our *"inner urge"* to develop our human potentiality into our spiritual actuality.

The ability to develop our potentiality into spiritual actuality is what I wish to address in this lesson. For movement from the potentiality of the flesh to the actuality of our spiritual nature is crucial to realizing our true essence. Realizing our true spiritual nature and power helps us answer the questions *"Who am I and why am I here?"*

Let us now examine the text and determine the lessons that will empower us to be all that God created us to be.

---

1)

The first lesson we learn about how to realize our true essence begins **_WHEN WE RECOGNIZE WHO WE ARE._** Read v1, *"See what love the Father has given us, that we should be called children of God; and so we are. The reason why the world does not know us is that it did not know him."(I Jn 3:1, RSV)*

The Letter of I John addressed a congregation that suffered a division among its members. Some of the members no longer believed that Jesus came in the flesh and John declares their views as instruments of evil. John tries to reassure his readers that they are the faithful ones and that those who have left the fold are the unfaithful ones. The Letter appears to be a family squabble and members have taken sides. John wants his followers to know that they are the true Children of God because they have continued to be faithful to the teachings of Christ.

In 1 John 3:1 we are told that we are *Children of God. (RSV)* This is a title we received not because of something we have done or by some act that has qualified us to be called *Children of God.* No, this description was lavished upon us because God the Father first loved us. In other words, this description, *Children of God,* instills in us the potential to accomplish and achieve anything and everything that we put our minds to do. *(I Jn 3:2, RSV)*

There is no one more capable than you are of reaching greatness. Each of you has the potential to be great at whatever your heart desires. Why? Because we are *Children of God!* Our motivation should be to develop the spark of potentiality that was placed in us when we accepted Jesus the Christ as Lord. *(I Jn 5:14-15, RSV)*

Your gifts are not my gifts, and my gifts may not be your gifts, but each of us has a gift that is couched in our potential to achieve whatever we strive to do. *(I Tim 4:14-15, RSV)*

---

2)

Our next lesson from the text teaches us that when we **_DEVELOP OUR POTENTIAL WE BECOME LIKE GOD._** Read v2,*"Beloved, we are God's children now; it does not yet appear what we shall be, but we know that when he appears we shall be like him, for we will see him as he is."(I Jn 3:2, RSV)*

I John balanced a promise of its readers' status as God's children now, with a reminder that the future into which they are growing had not been revealed. What the Church will be when Jesus returns is not for us to know. Paul reminds us in Romans 8:28, *"We know that in everything God works for good with those who love him, who are called according to his purpose." (RSV)*

God is love and how we see God is driven by God's love for us and our love for him and our neighbor. *(I Jn 4:7, RSV)* If we love God we need not worry about the persecution of this world because they did not know Jesus, they do not recognize us as *Children of God.* Yet we still need to maximize our potential as *Children of God.* This will steady us until Jesus returns. We may feel inferior or powerless in our times of need, but I John reminds us that we were created in the image of God. Therefore, we can become like God and see him for ourselves. *(I Jn 3:2, RSV)*

According to Aristotle every change in nature is a transformation of substance from potential to the actual. Therefore, nothing happens by chance. Everything that we experience daily, contributes to our realizing our true self. All of life's challenges prepare us for when we finally meet God face to face. (James L. Christian. *Philosophy: An Introduction to the Art of Wondering*, 7th edition. Holt, Rhinehart and *Winston*, Publishers. Fort Worth: 1998, p 80-84)

God gave us potentiality when God made us a "living soul." *(Gen 2:7b, RSV)* It is up to you and me to work it, mold it, prune it, expose it, promote it, and cherish it. Do not be like the man with only l talent who was afraid to work his talent, so he buried it until the master returned. Because he failed to work his potential, he was sentenced to eternal death. *(Mt 25:24, RSV)* Jesus tells us, *"We must work the works of him who sent me, while it is day; night comes, when no one can work." (Jn 9:4, RSV)*

---

3)

The third lesson to realizing our true essence is ***FINDING HOPE IN OUR DESTINY.*** Read v3, *"And everyone who thus hopes in him purifies himself, just as he is pure." (I Jn 3:3, RSV)*

As *Children of God,* we inherit two traits: doing *righteousness* and obtaining *purity. (I Jn 3:3, RSV)* In this context purity means *"moral rightness." (I Jn 3:7b, RSV)* For John if we are called *Children of God* then there should be some resemblance between God our Father, and his offspring. The world is looking for the connection between the two. The world does not know Jesus and unless we demonstrate his righteousness and love, we are not exhibiting our newly found DNA. *(I Jn 4:12, RSV)*

Now that our hope is grounded in our spiritual identity, we are purified through faith in the risen Christ. Our faith inspires and encourages us to reach our potentiality in this world so that we may bring others into the family of God. Whatever our current plight in life, we are not discouraged but find strength in whose we are and how far we can reach because of potentiality. Paul tells us in Philippians 4:13, *"I can do all things in him who strengthens me." (RSV)* That reassures us that there is nothing impossible for God to do through us and for us. *(Lk 1:37, RSV)* That is the hope that purifies us so that we can reflect the essence of God in our lives.

Yet, because we are still developing our potentiality in the flesh, we move forward with the hope that our potentiality will one day be actualized through the Spirit's intervention. In other words, how have we used our divine spark to reach our life goals? It will be our physical potentiality – what we do for Christ – that will motivate us to realize our spiritual actuality.

Therefore, as *Children of God* we move daily toward our divine origin in order to reach perfection. As *Children of God* our hope is to be just like God pure and righteous in love. Our true essence does not consist of unrighteousness and acts of destruction. But rather our true essence lies in the human faculty known as reason. Isaiah 1:18 reads, *"Come now, and let us reason together..." (KJV)* Then Paul tells us in Romans 12:2, *"Do not be conformed to this world, but be transformed by the renewal of your mind, that you may prove what is the will of God – what is good and acceptable and perfect."(RSV)*

As people of God, it is in our thinking that we participate in the perfection of God. Nothing else God made can reason, or engage in logic, but human beings. That is why we are created in his image. This is what makes us different from the animals, the plants, the rocks and trees. Our minds are a part of the Great Mind of the Universe – GOD. Therefore, we must be careful what we allow to enter our minds. *(Phil 4:8, RSV)*

The mind needs to be protected from the garbage of this world – negative influences that divide us. Unless we resist the world's mental garbage, we will never reach our full potentiality as *Children of God*. It is only through God that we can achieve our individual destinies here on earth. Only through the help of our Savior, Jesus the Christ, the righteous, can we realize our true essence of being. For he has called us *Children of God!* What higher title can we achieve, what greater honor can we receive?

We will never realize our full destiny without our spiritual connection to the Creator God who made each of us in his image, with a purpose and mission to complete and achieve before we leave this earth. The sooner we tap into this spiritual connection, the sooner our true essence will be realized and the better our lives will be. God bless you!

THE SECOND LETTER FROM JOHN

Guilty By Association

BEWARE OF THE COMPANY YOU KEEP!

2 JOHN: 7-11, *"For many deceivers have gone out into the world, men who will not acknowledge the coming Jesus Christ in the flesh; such a one is the deceiver and the antichrist! Look to yourselves, that you may not lose what you have worked for, but may win a full reward. Anyone who goes ahead and does not abide in the doctrine of Christ, does not have God; he who abides in the doctrines has both the Father and the Son." (RSV)*

INTRODUCTION

The second letter of John is a document that adopts the classic form of an ancient letter. It has a salutation, a thanksgiving, and a farewell. Tradition connects 2 John with both I John and the Gospel of John. The letter is addressed to the *"Elect Lady,"* a reference to the Church, which is feminine.

The reason for writing the letter is that there is a threat imposed by certain *"deceivers"* who deny that Jesus Christ has come in the flesh. *(II Jn 1:7, RSV)* It appears to be written some 60 years after Christ's return to the Father, when many mystery religions and philosophies were present.

Second John gives witness to a standard of correct doctrine and teaching that those who called themselves Christians must adhere to, and accept, if they want to be called *Children of God*. They could not just believe anything or everything that was being said in the name of the Church! Instead they were to stay true to the teachings they received from the Apostles: that Jesus was born of the virgin Mary, grew up in Nazareth, was baptized in the Jordan River by John the Baptizer, performed many signs and miracles via the power of God in his life. *(II Jn 1:9, RSV)*

Then Jesus was falsely accused, arrested, crucified, and buried *in* a borrowed tomb. *(Mt 27, RSV)* On the third day he arose from dead and ascended to the Father. *(Mt 28:7, RSV)* Yet, Jesus did not leave us alone. On the day of Pentecost, Jesus and the Father sent the Holy Spirit as our Comforter. *(Acts 2:1-4, RSV)* This is what the earlier Christians accepted as the gospel truth, no more, no less. Eventually it was put into a creed of faith known today as the *Apostles' Creed*. New converts were taught this creed and took a vow to believe it, practice it, and share it with all they encountered.

The sender of this letter is called the *"Elder."* (II Jn 1:1, RSV) This title can refer to a man of advanced years or a holder of an administrative position. The Elder speaks as one who has the authority to advise, even to threaten. The Elder of 2 John acknowledged that the congregation had received the anointing of the Holy Spirit. Therefore, the Elder encouraged the Church to hold on to the unadulterated word of God and not allow any false doctrine to penetrate the truth of the Gospel message they had received.

The audience is not just one lady but aimed at a Christian community meeting in a home of one of the believers. The *Lady's Children* refers to members of the Church. The two themes of this letter are *love* and *truth*. The command to *love* one another is prominent. *Truth* is the foundation within which the Elder's love for his Church is activated; and the condition by which they all will continue to be the Church of God. Truth is that vital Christian underlying force that empowers all who love. In order to preserve truth and love we must *beware of the company we keep.*

Let us now examine 2 John and learn from the Elder why we must beware of the company we keep.

---

1)

The first lesson we learn is ***THERE ARE MANY DECIEVERS IN OUR MIDST.*** Read v7, *"For many deceivers have gone out into the world, men who will not acknowledge the coming of Jesus Christ in the flesh; such a one is the deceiver and the antichrist."*(II Jn 1:7, RSV)

2 John emphasizes that the Church is a family – an *"Elect Lady and her Children."* (II Jn 1:1, RSV) As a family unit, the Church protects its members from lies, half-truths and misrepresentations of the true Gospel message. However, once Christianity became popular (*especially with the underclass, who saw the Church teach messages of hope, equality and love*) other religious groups sprang up and tried to piggyback and minimize the teachings of Christianity to create their own religion, and recruit members from the Christian Church family. They put their own theological spin on it to make it sound more palatable and less stringent on their daily lifestyles. *(II Jn 1:10, RSV)*

These imitators would include just enough Christian doctrine to lure believers away from the Church and into their interpretation of who Jesus was. Not everybody was on board with the Gospel message taught by the 12 disciples. Even Paul's teachings and preaching were tailored to his personal experience of the resurrected Christ because he did not know Jesus in the flesh. *(1 Cor 7:25, RSV)*

These variations of the Gospel truth concerned the Elder, so he takes the time to write to the Church because he has heard that the deceiver has infiltrated the Church and is trying to persuade the family that Jesus was not human, but merely a spirit who appeared to be in the flesh. This was totally contrary to the teachings of the Gospels and the disciples. *(II Jn 1:7, RSV)*

Matthew and Luke both record Jesus' human birth in order to counter this false teaching of Jesus' earthly origins. *(Mt 1:18-23; Lk 2:4-7, RSV)* John tells us that Jesus was with God in the beginning, but then he came and dwelt among us in the flesh. *(Jn 1:1-5,14, RSV)* That is what the word *Emmanuel* means – God with us! The Gospel of John directly confronts the deceiver's teachings.

The nonsense that this new religion taught claimed Jesus was not human. Therefore, he could not really experience what we go through in our lives. This teaching was to be rejected, rebuked, and denounced as the lie and falsehood that it was. The Elder then advised the Church to avoid those deceivers. They came to kill, to steal, and destroy the truth that they received when they accepted Jesus as Lord and Savior over their lives. *(Jn 10:10, RSV)*

The Elder's message rings so true today as well. We must beware of the many deceivers all around – at work, Church, play, family – anybody who is against the teaching of Jesus is the *"antichrist!" (I Jn 2:18, RSV)* Some will come as wolves in sheep clothing in order to gain our trust and confidence. *(Mt 7:15, RSV)* But Church let us beware for the Bible tells us to be as *"wise as serpents and innocent as doves." (Mt 10:16, RSV)*

Sometimes you may not be strong enough to resist the devil, so John tells us do not associate with evildoers in the first place! *(II Jn 1:10, RSV)* Instead beware of the company you keep.

———————————

2)

The second lesson we learn about why we should beware of the company we keep is ***BECAUSE YOU MAY END UP COMPROMISING YOUR FAITH.*** Read vv8-9, *"Look to yourselves, that you may not lose what you have worked for, but may win a full reward. Anyone who goes ahead and does not abide in the doctrine of Christ does not have God; he who abides in the doctrine has both the Father and the Son." (II Jn 1:8-9, RSV)*

The Elder's comments in 2 John, suggests that he is trying to head off another schism before it happens. In order to prevent this the Elder instructs the believers to continue to stay on guard less the things they were taught are lost, compromised, or dismissed. He warns the Church of what is at stake if they do not beware of the company they keep. *(II Jn 1:8, RSV)*

In verse 8 the Elder implies that he and others who know the truth have participated in their spiritual development. If they are not careful, they can lose all that they gained spiritually because of bad company and deceivers. They will try to corrupt the teachings of the early Apostles and twist the truth to their advantage. But if they stay faithful to the truth, they will receive a final reward when God calls his elect to enter the joy of the Master. *(Mt 25:21, RSV)*

Then in verse 9 the Elder argued that if anyone has moved beyond the teachings of the Gospels and denounced the foundational statement that Jesus came in the flesh, because they have accepted the false teachings of the deceivers, then these persons do not have God! *(II Jn 1:9, RSV)* In the words of the vernacular, *"You are a liar and truth is not in you!" (Jn 8:44, RSV)*

That is pretty much what the Elder said to the Church in his letter. You know the truth. Accept the truth! Hold on to the truth! Rebuke the deceiver for if you continue to abide in the teaching of Christ you get a package deal – the Father and the Son! *(II Jn 1:9, RSV)* So, beware of the company you keep! Our struggle is not against flesh and blood, but against the rulers, against the powers of this dark world and against spiritual forces of evil in the heavenly realm. *(Eph 6:12, RSV)*

As believers we try to mingle with non-believers to bring them into the kingdom of God. However, make sure your faith is strong enough *"to stand against the wiles of the devil"* by wearing the whole armor of God. *(Eph 6:11)* Make sure your faith holds and grips the rock of our faith, Jesus, the risen Christ. *(I Cor 10:4, RSV)* Do not allow the deceivers to convert you. Instead you take the lead and convert them. Shut down the deceivers and liars and expose them for who they are. Then beware of the company you keep.

---

3)

The final lesson we learn why we should beware of the company we keep is **_BECAUSE YOU WILL BE ACCUSED OF PARTICIPATING IN THEIR EVIL DEEDS._** Read vv10-11, *"If any one comes to you and does not bring this doctrine, do not receive him into the house or give him any greeting; for he who greets him shares his wicked work." (II Jn 1:10-11, RSV)*

The Elder in 2 John considered the situation at the Church a pervasive emergency touching on the fundamental confession of the nature of Jesus taught by the universal Church. To allow the deceivers to preach that Christ was never human, and was only a hologram, prevents the Christian from knowing the truth about God's power and love for his creation.

"The word became flesh and lived among us" is now under scrutiny! *(Jn 1:14, RSV)* They said that the Incarnation of Christ is a lie! They want to dismiss the Christmas story! This deeply concerned the Elder. For Christians would be unable to move forward without a tradition to remind them of whose they are, and where they have been.

Without Jesus, we are still sinners headed for a fiery ending. Jesus came to teach us what real love looks like. *(Jn 13:34, RSV)* If we join in with the naysayers and deceivers who reject his coming in the flesh, then we are just a lie away from committing the same evil behavior that caused Christ to come in the first place.

With Jesus as our role model, we are empowered to do the right thing. *(Heb 12:2, RSV)* When we accept Jesus as the Son of God who came in human form, we become candidates for the Holy Spirit. This Holy Spirit will sanctify us. This Holy Spirit will justify us. *(Jn 16:13, RSV)* This Holy Spirit sent to us by the Father and the Son will instill in us the Spirit of truth so that we want to do right, we want to talk right, we want to live right. *(Jn 15:26, RSV)*

Even though we fall, we get back up. Paul says, *"For I do not do the good I want, but the evil I do not want is what I do. Now if I do what I do not want, it is no longer I that do it, but sin that dwells within me." (Rom 7:19, RSV)* Therefore, try to avoid the presence of evil at every opportunity. None of us are perfect! Satan has no power over us. James tells us in 4:7, *"Resist the devil, and he will flee from you." (RSV)* So let us eliminate deceivers from our company. Then remember in the future to beware of the company you keep!

THE THIRD LETTER OF JOHN

Division In the Ranks

WHEN LEADERS DISAGREE

3 JOHN 1:9-10, *"I have written something to the Church; but Diotrephes, who likes to put himself first, does not acknowledge my authority. So if I come, I will bring up what he is doing, prating against me with evil words. And not content with that, he refuses himself to welcome the brethren, and also stops those who want to welcome them and puts them out of the Church."* *(RSV)*

INTRODUCTION

The third letter of John to this community Church was written for a specific occasion and addressed to a single person by the name of Gaius. This letter illustrates the kind of problems that arise in congregations when leaders do not agree and there is a power struggle.

Division arises and much chaos ensues as families and friends are forced to choose sides by denouncing one and promoting the other. These problems are no stranger to any organization but somehow the Church should be an exception. After all, we are told to love one another and walk in Jesus' truth. *(Jn 13:34, RSV)*

However, in our text this morning, that is not the case. Now let us listen as the Elder tries to counsel us on what to do *when leaders disagree.*

1)

The first lesson we learn why leaders disagree ***INVOLVES SELFISHNESS AND DISRESPECT FOR AUTHORITY.*** Read v9, *"I have written something to the Church; but Diotrephes, who likes to put himself first, does not acknowledge my authority." (III Jn 1:9, RSV)*

The letter is addressed to Gaius. Gaius is a common Roman name and perhaps serves in some capacity in the Johannine ministry in this city. The Elder claims authority over the congregation in this region as a bishop would do today in Churches that observe the episcopal hierarchy.

However, Diotrephes refused to acknowledge the Elder's authority and opposed any itinerant or traveling minister that comes to his town. *(III Jn 1:9-10, RSV)* The Elder described

Diotrephes as "putting himself first." This suggests that Diotrephes is a preacher and pastor who has chosen to abandon the rules and regulations of those in authority over him and dismissed anybody or anything that challenged his authority. *(III Jn 1:9, RSV)*

Perhaps the Elder and Diotrephes did not see eye to eye over how to pastor the Church he was assigned. Perhaps some disgruntled members contacted the Elder and complained about Diotrephes and Diotrephes felt no one had heard his side of the story. Perhaps he felt threatened and insecure when younger or more gifted ministers came to his town and drew a large crowd. *(III Jn 1:10, RSV)* We are not given the details in the scriptures, so we are left to our own imagination, in regards, to how these scenarios play out even today.

The Elder sent an earlier notice of a visiting minister coming to the Church, but Diotrephes ignored the communication. *(III Jn 1:9, RSV)* You see traveling preachers were dependent on the kindness of Christian congregations to house and feed them as they traveled throughout the region preaching and teaching God's word. There were no hotels or restaurants per se. Remember Luke 8 tells us that the women supported Jesus and his disciples as they traveled from town to town, region to region. *(Lk 8:2-3, RSV)*

In addition, the disciples were commissioned to go and take nothing with them. *(Mt 10:8-14, RSV)* Those whom they preached to were to welcome them with open hearts and arms. If they did not, that disciple was to shake the dust off their feet for a testimony against them. *(Mt 10:14; Mk 6:11, RSV)*

This is reminiscent of the experiences of African Americans in this country for decades after the Emancipation Proclamation. Whenever there were Church conferences or business meetings, African Americans were not allowed to stay in white hotels or eat in white restaurants. Church members in the towns where the conferences were held, opened their doors to the people attending the meetings, as well as prepared food for them to eat.

I remember as a child when we used to go to family reunions held in the southern states, my dad had to go to the back door of food joints and purchase sandwiches for us to eat in the car. We were not allowed to enter the restaurant. They wanted our money, but not our presence.

But it was all about Diotrephes. He did not want any preachers staying in his city. Maybe he was afraid they preached better or were better looking and might steal some of his members. Whatever the reason, Diotrephes is portrayed in the text as selfish, insecure, and had a problem with the Elder's authority over him. *(III Jn 9-10, RSV)*

As the Church, we are all have gifts and talents that make way for our survival and empower our purpose. There is no reason to ever be envious of somebody else's gift. Whatever you need to do in order to make your gift succeed, just do it! Maybe you need to go back to school and get another degree. Maybe you need to serve as an intern to learn the job or as an apprentice. There is no shame in serving under someone who has already obtained the level of success you want for your own life.

Do whatever it takes! Do not begrudge someone's success. Celebrate the person who can sing better than you can. Celebrate the preacher who has the gift of gab and the charisma of a Martin Luther King, Jr. Celebrate the cook who wins the blue ribbon every time. Then when you obtain your success, remember to give God the praise and the glory. Remember to put God first, and credit God for your gift that will direct your purpose. God will share his glory with no one. *(Isa 42:8, RSV)*

Therefore, do not be selfish and think it is all about you, because it is not. Do not be arrogant for *"pride goes before destruction, and a haughty spirit before a fall." (Prov 16:18, RSV)* Remember to treat everybody as a child of God. *(Gal 6:10, RSV)* We are all equal in the eyes of God. When we put God first, all the blessings from heaven will fall freely in our direction. However, if we try to make it about us, that not only opens the door to chaos, but it will cause conflict with leaders who disagree with you.

_____

2)

Our second lesson reveals that leaders disagree because ***FALSE RUMORS HAVE BEEN SPREAD ABOUT THEM.*** Read v10a, *"So if I come, I will bring up what he is doing, prating against me with evil words." (III Jn 1:10a, RSV)*

Diotrephes was spreading false malicious slander against the Elder to destroy his reputation and undermine his authority over the community at large. *(III Jn 1:10, RSV)* The Elder has accused him of works and words that are evil. James 3:8 says, *"But no human being can tame the tongue- a restless evil, full of deadly poison." (RSV)*

But why is Diotrephes so angry with the Elder? Was there a butting of heads over theological issues or socio-political concerns? There was a breakdown somewhere in the relationship and Diotrephes and the Elder disagreed to the point that Diotrephes felt the need to spread vicious rumors about the Elder! Diotrephes needed to show his authority over his congregation by personally degrading the Elder – his beliefs and practices – and chose to speak evil instead of doing good. *(III Jn 1:11, RSV)*

They say that there is no hurt like Church hurt. We are told to forgive and love one another, and that love covers a multitude of sins. *(I Peter 4:8, RSV)* There was a breakdown in the family of God! Whenever that happens, whenever leaders disagree, nobody wins. The body of Christ is wounded. Then only the Holy Spirit can bring reconciliation to the family.

Jesus taught us how to resolve conflict between believers. Go to the one who you have wronged and ask for their forgiveness first. *(Mt 5:23-24)* Then go to God in prayer. James 4:11 reads, *"Do not speak evil against one another, brethren."(RSV)* Again James 1:26 says, *"If anyone thinks he is religious, and does not bridle his tongue, but deceives his heart, this man's religion is vain."(RSV)* In the words of the former first lady, Michelle Obama, ""*When they go low, we go high.*"

Yes, leaders will disagree. But we should never be disagreeable and resort to character assassination and malicious slander. Instead let us come together and learn from one another. This is true with cultural, racial, and gender differences as well. In the words of an old Native American proverb, *"Don't judge me until you have walked a mile in my shoes."* In other words, empathy should be the rule of the day, not the exception to the rule. When we leave empathy out of the equation, and only want our way, leaders will disagree.

3)

The final lesson we learn from our text tells us that leaders disagree when ***THERE IS A STRUGGLE FOR POWER.*** Read v10b, *"And not content with that, he refuses himself to welcome the brethren, and also stops those who want to welcome them and puts them out of the Church."(III Jn 1:10b, RSV)*

Wow! Diotrephes is so opposed to the Elder and the Johannine community, that he will not even entertain a fellow believer in his Church and prevents anyone in his congregation from hosting a believer as well! If they do, Diotrephes threatened to excommunicate them! *(III Jn 1:10, RSV)*

It was not enough that Diotrephes was spreading malicious gossip about the Johannine community, now he has gone so far as to ban any of them from stepping foot in his Church! James 1:20 reads, *"For the anger of man does not work the righteousness of God." (RSV)*

There is some serious disagreeing going on here to take such drastic measures to prevent other believers from visiting your Church. What caused such fear in Diotrephes' heart and mind? Was his doctrine and theology so radically different from the Elder's teachings that any contact was a threat to his authority?

Perhaps Diotrephes practiced a less rigorous doctrine of how Christians ought to behave and what they ought to believe. Every believer did not necessarily believe the same thing as we see in the four Gospels and denominationalism today. Diotrephes was protecting his *"turf"* and had complete control over his local Church situation. He was not going to allow anyone to disturb the mental and spiritual hold he had on his membership.

The Church has been divided since the post-apostolic period – a period when all 12 disciples and Paul are no longer alive. Different doctrines and philosophies have now infiltrated the Church at a rapid pace. Trying to piggy-back on the success of the Christian movement, some religious leaders, who thought the teachings of Christ were too strict, or not strict enough, attracted believers into their folds.

During the fourth century, Emperor Constantine of Rome, held 7 Council meetings in order to get the Church on the same page about doctrine and religious practices. However, he failed and caused even more division because the majority ruled and the minority felt alienated, so they left the established Church and created their own.

Later, some were declared heretics and were met with violence, forcing them to summit to the majority's perspective on the Christian belief system. Others went underground and refused to reunite with the majority Church. This was how the Protestant Church eventually came to life. Leaders disagreed because of greed and a struggle for power, not for the cause of Christ.

Today, in the 21st century, religious leaders still disagree. We have mega-churches that have attracted many members from the traditional Churches. They have disagreed with the doctrines of the official Church universal and instituted new ways and practices for doing religion and following Christ.

Yes, leaders will and do disagree, but how does that affect the sinner? Are they shopping around from Church to Church to satisfy their own comfort zone? What are they willing to give up in order to follow Christ? This is nothing new. The Pharisees and Sadducees, Essenes and Zealots, disagreed in Jesus' day. Jesus saw the disunity and religious divide and tried to bring the people together with one law, *"that you love one another; even as I have loved you..."* *(John 13:34, KJV)*

When we get this law right, leaders will still disagree but without hatred and revenge in their hearts. Leaders will seek God's face and come together under the sacrificial banner of Jesus the Christ. No one will be arrogant. No one will spread false rumors and try to tear their fellow believers down because they have different opinions. No one will struggle for power because they will accept that power comes from the Holy Spirit. For the prophet Zechariah stated, *"Not by might, nor by power, but by my Spirit, says the Lord of hosts." (Zech 4:6, RSV)*

When that day comes truly Jesus will mount his white horse and return to claim his own who will live with him throughout all eternity in a place where we can all agree to crown him Lord of Lords, and King of Kings! God bless you!

A LETTER FROM JUDE

When Hope is Built On Faith

GOD'S HELP, OUR HOPE

JUDE 1:24-25, *"Now to him who is able to keep you from falling, and to present you without blemish before the presence of his glory with rejoicing, to the only God, our Savior through Jesus Christ our Lord, be glory, majesty, dominion, and authority, before all time and now and forever. Amen." (RSV)*

INTRODUCTION

Not many people have read the Letter of Jude. Those who have cannot remember if it is in the Old Testament or the New Testament. It is a little book – has only one chapter – and is located near the end of the New Testament, just before the Book of Revelation.

Although Jude is a small letter compared to Corinthians and Romans, its message and purpose is indispensable to the Christian faith and practice. For you see Jude was writing in response to the false teachings going around called *Docetism*. Docetism taught that Jesus was not human, only divine. Therefore, it implied that what we do daily as human beings, is not important, only your soul must give an account for your life here on earth.

This of course is and always will be an untruth. Christ was fully human and fully divine. He cried just like we cry. *(Jn 11:35, RSV)* He hurt just like we hurt. *(Mk 15:19, RSV)* He felt lonely just like we feel lonely at times. *(Mk 15:34, RSV)* Yet even though he was prone to human feelings, Christ was able to conquer his flesh and we can too.

Docetism is a cop out and misinterpretation of God's word and Jesus' life. It is an excuse for not trying to do the right thing. Christianity is a moral and ethical religion because our leader, our head, Jesus the Christ, was and is a moral and ethical Savior. He taught us to love and care for one another. This love should manifest itself in how we care for the least of our society. *(Mt 25:40-, RSV)*

Jesus was as much concerned for our physical bodies as he was for our spiritual souls. Jesus came to make us whole – mind, body and soul – allowing the soul and the body to give in to God's will.

Let us now listen for Jude's message of hope that is directly connected to God's will for our lives.

1)

The first lesson we learn from our text is **_GOD IS ABLE!_** Read v 24a, *"Now to him who is able…" (Jude 1:24, RSV)*

When we think of someone being able, we imagine that person to have unlimited abilities, resources, and powers. Nothing is too hard for them. They are always consistent, reliable, and dependable. You can always count on that person to get the job done.

For Jude, this was the profile of God as taught by the disciples. God can see through any and every situation. Our ancestors understood and believed that slavery would one day be a thing of the past and freedom to live in America as equal citizens would become a reality for their children. The slave master could never destroy their dream of one day being free because they believed in a God who was able to do all things if they believed! However, in their wildest dreams, they never imagined a Black President of the United States of America! God is true to his word.

In our society today, we still suffer from the same heresies of the early Church. We still – like Jude- must refute the lies and impurities of false teachers and prophets in order to keep our faith from being watered down. *(Jude 1:4, RSV)* Unfortunately, many Church members have already been infected. You remember how zestful you were when you first found the Lord. The heresies and lies of Satan that have infiltrated the word of God have caused us to become divided. *(Jude 1:4, RSV)* They have stolen our fire.

This is what Jude is trying to prevent from happening to the Church. He knew the powers that were strong and influential, but he also knew that God is able. *(Jude 1:24a, RSV)* All we can do is trust him and believe that God will do what his word promises he will do.

2)

The second lesson we learn from the Letter of Jude is **_FALLING IS NOT AN OPTION!_** "Read v 24b, *"…to keep you from falling." (Jude 1:24b, RSV)*

Jude writes this letter to encourage the recipients to remain faithful and to lead virtuous lives. They are to reject the immoral lure of false teachers who are preying upon the Christian community. Jude was a blood brother of James and a servant of Christ. *(Jude 1:1, RSV)* The false teachers where trying to lead the faithful astray with their moral laxity. Second Peter also used the letter from Jude when arguing the necessity of living a moral and righteous life before the world. *(2 Peter 2:21-22, RSV))*

Therefore, when Jude speaks of God *keeping us from falling*, he is making a reference to sin and returning to the life we lived before we were saved, baptized, and filled with the Holy Spirit. *(Jude 1:17, RSV)* Jude is also making a reference to our falling out of love with both God and our neighbor. *(Jude 1:21, RSV)* We may make mistakes and take a wrong turn every now and then on this spiritual journey, but God has our back! God will keep us from falling because his Son, our Lord and Savior, is our safety net. When we mess up, we have an Advocate with the Father and that is Jesus Christ the righteous. *(I Jn 2:1, RSV)* God's Holy Word gives us direction that leads us back to God. David says, *"Thy word is a lamp to my feet and a light to my path." (Ps 119:105, KJV)*

As long as we remain in the flesh and choose to live immoral lives, falling is an option, especially if we do not love God with all our hearts, minds, bodies and souls, and our neighbor as ourselves. *(Lk 10:27, RSV)* But when we acknowledge his power, his love, we cannot fall from his grace and mercy. Christ's power covers us if we only have faith the size of a mustard seed. *(Mt 17:20, RSV)* Yes, we fall, but we get up!

---

3)

The third lesson from our text teaches us that ***OUR STANDING BEFORE GOD IS GOOD!*** Read v24c, *"... to present you without blemish before the presence of his glory with rejoicing." (Jude 1:24c, RSV)*

Now because God is able to keep us from falling, God is also able to present us faultless before his presence with exceeding joy! *(Jude 1:24c, RSV)* Jude concludes his argument by urging the community to strengthen their faith through prayer and to be rooted in God's love, counting on God's mercy and grace to sustain them until the second coming of Christ. *(Jude 1:20-21, RSV)* Jude gives them instructions to support those who are weak in the faith so they will not fall prey to the immoral teachings presented to them by false teachers. *(Jude 1:7-8, RSV)* Their standing before God is connected both to their moral behavior and their faith. The two go hand in hand.

This verse is part of the doxology Jude composed as a spiritual farewell in his letter. *(Jude 1:24, RSV)* As he came to the end of his letter, he reminds the reader that God's power and authority are before all time, now and forever. *(Jude 1:25, RSV)* There is no getting around it. We come to God through Jesus Christ our Lord and not through some false practice or ritual that the false teachers are selling. *(Jn 14:6, RSV)* Jesus was born of a woman, suffered, died, and rose again on the third day. This is the Christian's truth and badge of honor, to know our God loved us so much that he would allow his only begotten Son to die for our sins. *(Jn 3:16, RSV)*

Then when we acknowledge that God is able, to keep us from falling, and to present us faultless in his presence, we come before him with rejoicing and praise and honor and glory and thanksgiving. *(Jude 1:24b, RSV)* God has done it all to preserve us until the end of time. God has covered us with the sacrifice of his Son so that our standing before him is good. All our past sins have been forgiven. All our shortcomings are dismissed. There is no accuser to call judgment on us. That is the reason we rejoice!

God is our help and our only hope. *(Ps 46:1, RSV)* We thought better education would change the world, but it did not. We thought better economic conditions would do it, well that did not work either. We tried everything and everything has failed to change the evil cold hearts of humanity. Racism, classism, sexism, are still prominent stains on our society today as it was 2020 years ago. Therefore, God is our only hope. Everything else comes up short.

Having a right relationship with God and living lives that are acceptable in his sight now is all one needs to keep from falling in this life and stand faultless before him in the world to come. God bless you!

APOCALYPTIC LITERATURE

THE BOOK OF REVELATION

Apocalyptic Literature: A New Heaven and a New Earth

THE DOORWAY TO ETERNAL LIFE

REVELATION 21:4, *"...He will wipe away every tear from their eyes, and death shall be no more, neither shall there be mourning nor crying nor pain any more, for the former things have passed away." (RSV)*

INTRODUCTION

The book of Revelation is the most difficult book in the New Testament to understand. It is full of symbols, elaborate imagery, and religious mysteries most of which the original meanings have been lost through time. It was written during a time, when the Roman officials persecuted the early Christians because they refused to worship idol gods.

In order to avoid persecution and detection, the early Christians wrote in code language so that the Roman officials would not know that they were sending messages to their members. If they were caught, they would have been tried for treason, a crime punishable by death. This is how the symbolism and codes became so popular.

The author of Revelation was a Christian named John the Divine. He wrote not as the originator of the material or as its author, but rather as a secretary taking dictation from God. *(Rev 1:11, RSV)* John declared that he was in the Spirit on the Lord's Day when he heard a loud voice like a trumpet saying, *"Write what you see in a book and send it to the seven Churches..."* *(Rev 1:11, RSV)* So John is recording as a witness to what will happen in the new age, when God will create a new heaven and a new earth. *(Rev 21:1, RSV)*

The words of John the Divine are pertinent to every Christian as he gives us lessons on how to walk through the doorway to eternal life.

1)

The first lesson from the text is **GOD SEES OUR PAIN.** Read v 4, *"He will wipe away every tear from their eyes." (Rev 21:4, RSV)*

John described what it would be like in the new heaven and the new earth. God will dwell among humans again like he did with Adam and Eve in the Garden of Eden. *(Gen 3:8, RSV)* The prophets of the Old Testament often warned that God would destroy this present world because of the level of sin that existed in his creation. *(Zeph 1:1-3, RSV)* God did it once in the days of Noah and now is about to do it again. This plan of *recreation* was shown to John while on the island of Patmos. The level of wickedness had surpassed even God's mercy and grace. It was time to start over, fresh and new, with people who were committed to God's will and authority. *(Rev 1:1, RSV)*

John the Divine's punishment for preaching the Word of God was to be exiled on the Island of Patmos. *(Rev 1:9, RSV)* It was while on this Island that this great revelation was given to him so John would know that God had not forsaken his people and God saw the sufferings they were experiencing because of his Son's teachings.

This is the same sentiment that God expressed to Moses on the mountain. *(Exo 3:1, RSV)* God told Moses that he had heard the cries of his people in Egyptian slavery and now was sending Moses as the deliverer on his behalf. *(Exo 3:7-8, RSV)* This lets us know that even during our darkest days and loneliness nights, God is there with us and for us, even when it does not feel like it.

John the Divine tells us there is a day, a new age coming where we will not have to cry anymore. God is going to wipe all tears away. *(Rev 21:4, RSV)* We will no longer be caught or tricked by Satan's traps because Satan will no longer be around. In the new heaven and the new earth, Satan and his demons will be banished, and everlasting joy will replace the hours once spent in weeping. *(Rev 20:2-3, RSV)*

So, for John to say specifically that *"God will wipe away every tear from their eyes"* portrays a level of comfort and concern that we all can relate to. *(Rev 21:4, RSV)* Many of us have cried ourselves to sleep at night not knowing what tomorrow will bring. In our daily life, there always seems to be something trying to push us to tears. Perhaps a harsh and unkind word is said. Maybe an anniversary or birthday is forgotten, sickness, accidents, even the death of a loved one, all these things crowd our lives and sometimes overwhelm us to the point of tears.

Yet, even though sometimes we have to cry, we believe the words of the Psalmist, *"Weeping may tarry for the night, but joy comes with the morning."(Ps 30:5, KJV)* God's revelation as to how deeply God feels our pain reassures believers that God will have the last say.

---

2)

Our second lesson promises us that ***THE SUFFERINGS OF THE FLESH WILL BE CANCELLED!*** Read v 4b, *"and death shall be no more, neither shall there be mourning nor crying nor pain anymore..." (Rev 21:4b, RSV)*

John sees the Holy City descending out of heaven. *(Rev 21:2, RSV)* That which descends from heaven is a blessing rather than a curse on humanity, as some past cities have been towards Jerusalem (Babylon, *2 Kgs 24:10-11, RSV*); Rome, *Acts 18:2, RSV*). The Holy City is a place where people will flock to, not run away from for fear of their lives. God has promised to be with them, and God's very presence will reflect joy, happiness, forgiveness, and thanksgiving.

As we begin to experience a new heaven and a new earth, we are now new creations. Our status is not in the flesh, but in the spirit. We will be inoculated against death, sorrow, and pain in our new status and transformation. In fact, there will be nothing to cry about, nothing to mourn over, for death was conquered on the cross and Jesus will now relate to us as spiritual beings, not human beings. *(Rev 20:14; 21:4, RSV)*

In this life we know from birth that one day we must die. We know that we are only promised 70 years and everything beyond that is "borrowed time" as we say in the African American Church. *(Ps 90:10, RSV)* We work and plan all our lives preparing for the day when we will meet our Creator. However, we know we will not see death until our race on earth is completed. *(2 Tim 4:7, RSV)*

Yet knowing one day we will have to leave this world, sorrow and mourning are still a part of our emotional tool bag when someone close to us passes away. Paul tells us in I Thessalonians 4:13-14 that we do not mourn as those who have no hope, because we know our hope is in the resurrected Christ. *(RSV)* Christ promised to come back for us and to take us back with him to heaven where we will experience eternal life. *(Jn 14:3, RSV)* This promise lightens the sorrow, and we look forward to the day that we will see our loved ones again. For death is the doorway to eternal life.

---

3)

Our final lesson from this text teaches us that **_WE SHOULD LET GO OF THE PAST._** Read v4c, *"for the former things have passed away." (Rev 21:4c, RSV)*

God does not say that he is making new all things, but rather he is making all things new. There is a difference. One can refurbish something that is already in use or recycle something for a new purpose. But God is not saying that. God is telling John that what he did in the beginning, the first things – creation – is now cancelled! It is all in the past because it has all succumb to sin, corruption and wickedness. *(Rev 21:5, RSV)* The first stuff is unacceptable for the new heaven and the new earth.

As Christians, many of us expect life to be rosy and pleasant most of the time. Then when something negative happens in our lives, we question God by asking "why me?" John tells us that when the new heaven and the new earth are created, only then can we declare, *"The former things have passed away." (Rev 21:4d, RSV)* As long as we live in this world and this age, evil will always be present. Before we can expect life to go smoothly, this world must pass away. Sickness and death, trials and tribulations, are a permanent part of this world. But when Jesus comes back all former things shall pass away. *(Rev 22:11-13, RSV)*

This old world must be *recreated*! Jesus will gather up all who served him in this world and take them to the place he has gone to prepare for them. *(Jn 14:2-3, RSV)* Those who have died in Christ shall rise-up at the sound of the trumpet. *(I Th 4:16, RSV)* Death for them is the doorway to a better life – life eternal. We all want to be in that number that no one can number because it is too large to calculate by the human mind. *(Rev 7:9, RSV)* But to be included in that number, one must be invited to the marriage supper of the Lamb. *(Rev 19:9, RSV)*

There is a story about a truck driver who was driving across the country. He got one-fourth the way across and his tires blew out. He got them replaced. He got half-way across and the radiator and fuel pump broke. He got them fixed. Finally, he made it to his destination.

A week later he started his journey back home. Before he got out of the state the truck caught on fire and the body of the truck was badly burned. The truck driver called up his boss and told him about the fire and how the body of the truck was destroyed. His boss asked him about the engine. He said the engine was just fine. The boss told him to then junk the body but ship the engine back home.

That is what happens when death knocks at our door. This human body is junked, and the soul is sent back to God. Death is the doorway to eternal life if you live for God while your body is still in-tact. God bless you!

REFERENCES

Interpreter's Dictionary of the Bible. Vols 1-5, Abingdon Press: Nashville, 1976

The Anchor Bible Dictionary. Freedman, David, Noel, editor-in-chief. Doubleday: New York, 1992

The Holy Bible, RSV, KJV

The Interpreter's Bible. Vols 1-12, Abingdon Press: New York, 1953

The New Century Bible Commentary. Marshal, Morgan, and Scott. Ltd; London, 1971

The New Interpreter's Bible. Vols 1-12. Abingdon: Nashville, 1995

The New Interpreter's Bible. NRSV with Apocrypha. Abingdon Press: Nashville, 1995

The New Testament Study Bible. NRSV. Vols 1-20, The Complete Biblical Library: Springfield, 1986

The World Biblical Commentary. Word Books: Waco, 1988

Printed in the United States
By Bookmasters